I flopped down on the folding canvas cot, adjusted the mosquito net around me, and zonked out. <u>Blamm!</u> I jerked awake. At first I thought it was the nearby battery of 155 howitzers firing a little interdiction. <u>Kerboom-wham-bang!! Snap-pop-crack</u> . . . Slugs ripped through the wire screen over my head. Holy shit, I thought, automatically rolling off my cot to the hard cement floor, that's <u>incoming!</u>

One of the corner machine guns opened up, and it sounded like the gunner fired off the entire 250-round belt in a single burst. "Get to the outer walls!" someone yelled. "Get your weapons and get a firing position!"

"They're coming through the front gate!" another voice outside yelled, sending chills up my spine. . . .

Books published by The Ballantine Publishing Group are available at quantity discounts on bulk purchases for premium, educational, fund-raising, and special sales use. For details, please call 1-800-733-3000.

Tan Phu

Special Forces Team A-23 in Combat

Leigh Wade

IVY BOOKS • NEW YORK

Ivy Books
Published by Ballantine Books
Copyright © 1997 by Leigh Wade

http://www.randomhouse.com

Library of Congress Catalog Card Number: 96-94967

ISBN 0-8041-1616-4

Manufactured in the United States of America

First Edition: April 1997

10 9 8 7 6 5 4 3 2 1

*Battle is the most magnificent competition
in which a human being can indulge.*
—GEN. GEORGE S. PATTON

*It is well that war is so terrible,
or we should grow too fond of it.*
—GEN. ROBERT E. LEE

*Great horror as war itself is, every
honest soldier knows that it has its
moments of joy.*
—GEN. MATTHEW B. RIDGWAY

Preface

I went to Vietnam the first time in 1963 and was there off and on until 1971. For me personally, there were several distinct phases to the conflict, each with its own flavor. I've always remembered the beginning of my involvement in Vietnam as being more exciting, more *fun*, than the latter periods. This was not, as some might think, because things were easier then.

In those early days we had none of the luxurious air, artillery, or logistical support that was common later on. Nor were there any large American infantry units to come running to our aid when we got in over our heads. Hell, there wasn't even any Mike Force! No, the war wasn't easy on a Special Forces A-team in the early sixties, and at a place like Camp Tan Phu, it was pretty rough.

Still, there was just something about it that made it more fun. Probably because I was young then, and war is really a young man's game.

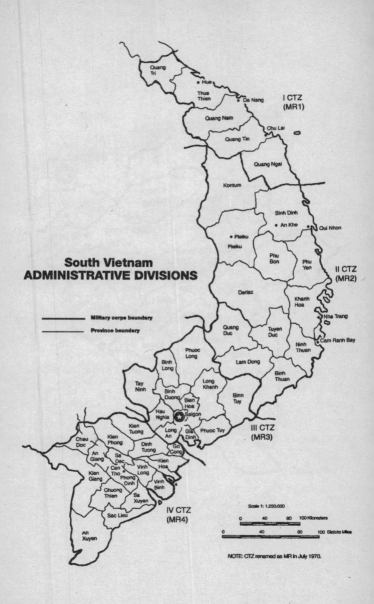

South Vietnam
ADMINISTRATIVE DIVISIONS

——— Military corps boundary

——— Province boundary

Quang Tri

• Hue

Thua Thien

• Da Nang

I CTZ (MR1)

Quang Nam

Chu Lai

Quang Tin

Quang Ngai

Kontum

Binh Dinh

• An Khe

Qui Nhon

• Pleiku

Pleiku

Phu Bon

Phu Yen

II CTZ (MR2)

Darlac

Khanh Hoa

Nha Trang

Quang Duc

Tuyen Duc

Cam Ranh Bay

Ninh Thuan

Phuoc Long

Lam Dong

Binh Long

Long Khanh

Binh Thuan

Tay Ninh

Binh Duong

Bien Hoa

Binh Tuy

Hau Nghia

Saigon

Kien Tuong

Long An

Gia Dinh

Phuoc Tuy

III CTZ (MR3)

Chau Doc

Kien Phong

Dinh Tuong

Go Cong

An Giang

Sa Dec

Can Tho

Kien Hoa

Kien Giang

Phong Dinh

Vinh Long

Chuong Thien

Sa Xuyen

Vinh Binh

Sac Lieu

IV CTZ (MR4)

An Xuyen

Scale 1: 1,250,000

0   40   60   100 Kilometers

0   40   80   100 Statute Miles

NOTE: CTZ renamed as MR in July 1970.

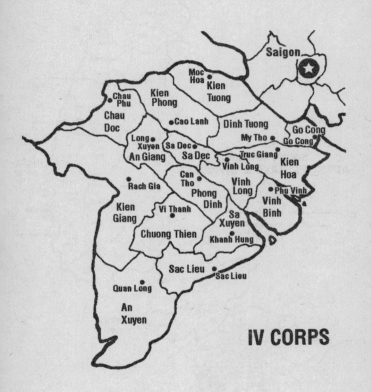

Saigon

Moc Hoa
Kien Tuong

Chau Phu
Kien Phong
Chau Doc

Cao Lanh
Dinh Tuong

Go Cong
Go Cong
My Tho

Long Xuyen
Sa Dec
An Giang
Sa Dec

Truc Giang
Vinh Long
Kien Hoa

Rach Gia
Can Tho
Phong Dinh
Vinh Long

Phu Vinh
Vinh Binh

Kien Giang
Vi Thanh
Sa Xuyen

Chuong Thien
Khanh Hung

Sac Lieu
Sac Lieu

Quan Long

An Xuyen

IV CORPS

AN XUYEN

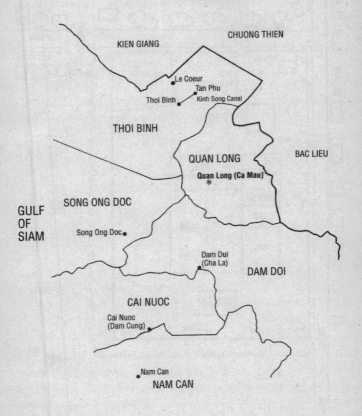

KIEN GIANG

CHUONG THIEN

Le Coeur
Tan Phu
Thoi Binh
Kinh Song Canal

THOI BINH

QUAN LONG

BAC LIEU

Quan Long (Ca Mau)

SONG ONG DOC

GULF
OF
SIAM

Song Ong Doc

Dam Dui
(Cha La)

DAM DOI

CAI NUOC

Cai Nuoc
(Dam Cung)

Nam Can

NAM CAN

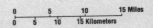

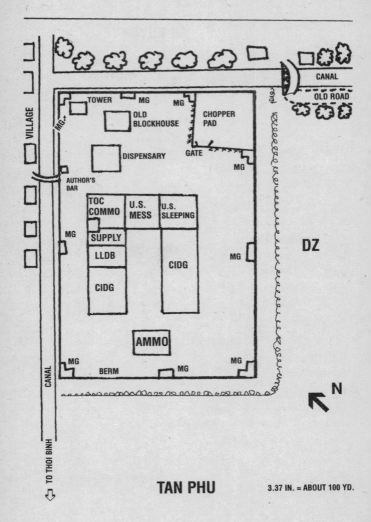

TAN PHU

3.37 IN. = ABOUT 100 YD.

Chapter 1

It was October 29, 1963. I was standing outside the palm thatch building that served as our operations center and was trying to talk on two PRC-10 radios at the same time. We had a large combat operation in heavy contact with the enemy, and there was an airdrop of supplies coming in I was trying to coordinate. Our demolitions sergeant, Bill Martin, was jumping in with the resupply.

"CV-2, this is Tan Phu," I said into one handset, talking to the Caribou aircraft, "move your release point to one hundred meters due west. You're putting the stuff in our wire, over."

"Rattlesnake One, this is Rattlesnake Nest," I said into the other handset, trying to contact the operation, "short count follows: one, two, three, four, five, five, four, three, two, one. This is Nest, over."

VandeBerg, our medic, was up in the tower yelling down to me. "You getting anything from Rowe and Pitzer? I can see airbursts and tracers!"

The CV-2 was making a lazy, low pass directly over the area where the battle was taking place. The cargo plane had an escort of one armed T-28, which was circling at a higher altitude. I was trying to radio the pilot of the Caribou to tell him to be careful of ground fire when I

1

saw the plane start taking evasive action. The pilot threw the coal to the engines. The CV-2 made one more low pass over our camp's drop zone at about seven hundred feet and Martin jumped. His chute just barely had time to open before he was in the rice paddy. The planes flew away, back toward Can Tho.

I was still holding the handsets of the PRC-10s to my ears when, very faintly, I heard Lieutenant Rowe's voice over the air/ground frequency. He was trying to contact the aircraft. "CV-2, CV-2, this is Tan Phu, over. . . ." His voice was calm and controlled, but I could still detect the urgency. I immediately attempted to contact him, but the channel was suddenly filled with whistling and jabbering in Vietnamese.

Captain Phil Arsenault, our detachment commander, came hurrying up. "Wade, you get that message to the B-team yet about the operation getting hit?"

I told him that Sergeant Sidney Cross, the other radio operator on our detachment, was in the commo bunker trying to get through to them. Our only connection with our higher headquarters and any outside help was through an AN/GRC-109 radio that had only fifteen watts of power and could only transmit Morse code.

"You contact Rowe yet?" the CO asked, visibly fuming. I told him I had no commo with them, but had just heard Rowe on the air/ground frequency. Arsenault cursed and stormed off to check with our Vietnamese Special Forces (LLDB) counterparts.

A unit of our Civilian Irregular Defense Group (CIDG) began closing into camp, and I saw that it was the fire-support element we had sent out with one of our 81mm mortars. Staff Sergeants John Lowe and Ponce Navarro, our two weapons men, were with them. "Big

John" and Ponce were unaware that the assault element
had come under attack. Wearing their web gear and still
carrying folding-stock carbines, they came over to where
I stood next to our outdoor jungle antenna. It was a typical hot, tropical morning, and their camouflage uniforms
were soaked with sweat.

"The last word we got from Lieutenant Rowe was
that it looked like another walk in the sun," Lowe said.
"So we followed the plan and came back in. What's
happening?"

Martin, covered with mud and slime from his landing
in the paddy, also staggered up. He threw down the kit
bag, which was filled with his heavy, wet parachute. "We
were taking ground fire!" he said, pointing over in the
direction of the beleaguered operation. "I told the pilot to
make one more pass, and I unassed. . . . You need to tell
the operation to watch out!"

I was trying to explain to all of them that the operation
was under attack, but that we had lost radio contact
with them. Suddenly there was a commotion from the
west gate. The first group of dead and wounded had
arrived. . . .

This ill-fated operation was the largest and most ambi-
tious one we had yet attempted at Tan Phu. Several of us
on the detachment, including Lieutenant Rowe, were
uneasy about it from the beginning. For being our largest
operation ever, it was thrown together very quickly—to
take advantage of some "hot intel" that Arsenault and
Captain Versace, a visiting officer from Military Assistance and Advisory Group (MAAG), had picked up
while on a visit to the district chief. I'd gotten the distinct

impression that one of the main reasons for the operation was to impress our guest.

According to the questionable intelligence report, a small unit of Cong was establishing a command post at the village of La Coeur. Our plan was to run a simple "hammer and anvil" operation in which an assault element pushes the enemy into a blocking force. The problems were many.

First of all, the village of La Coeur was farther away from camp than we had ever ventured. It was out of range of our camp mortars and was at the maximum range of our PRC-10 field radios. Another scary part of our plan was that we would be stretching our manpower resources to the maximum.

At that time we had only three fully equipped and trained strike force companies of approximately one hundred men each. We also had a fourth, all-Cambodian company of new recruits who were untrained, and as yet unarmed. We were not too certain of the loyalties of these Cambodians and were still in the process of checking them out prior to giving them weapons.

We were sending two full companies out on the operation, and also the heavy weapons platoon. This was over two-thirds of our effective camp strength. The Vietnamese Special Forces team had elected to send their entire command structure—their detachment commander, team sergeant, and intelligence sergeant—along with their senior medic, on the venture.

We'd known from the beginning that commo would be a problem, and the original plan was for me to accompany Rowe and Pitzer to handle it. But when the decision was made that Ponce and Lowe would also be going on the operation with the mortars, the plan was changed.

The unofficial rule was that no more than two Americans at a time would accompany any combat operation. We were already sending four, not counting Versace, so my LLDB counterpart, Dih Dah, would go instead.

On top of everything else, we were expecting a resupply drop the next morning, and that would require men for DZ security, labor parties to carry in and store the supplies, and someone to talk to the pilot of the aircraft. Bill Martin, who usually accompanied Rowe on all operations, had gotten wind of the upcoming action and had elected to parachute in with the resupply in an attempt to get back in time to go along.

That evening before the operation, I sat for a long time on top of a bunker with Dan Pitzer. As we watched the peaceful sunset, we talked about home and the future. Dan had seemed more talkative than normal. He told me of his plans to get out of Special Forces when we got back. He said he wanted to get in some easy racket like NCO club management for his few remaining years in the Army, and then start his own bar after he retired. It was my last conversation with Dan for a long time.

Cross stuck his head out of the commo bunker. "Someone get Captain Arsenault!" he yelled to me where I still stood by the jungle antenna, attempting to contact the operation. "I got the B-detachment commander standing by, and he wants to talk to our CO."

"What the fuck does he think a 109 radio is, a goddamned telephone?" I shouted to my fellow radio operator as I started over to the LLDB operations hooch. Cross just rolled his eyes in reply and disappeared back into the radio bunker. I found Arsenault and told him we had the B-team on the horn and that their commander wanted him to stand by the radio to keep them updated on our situation.

"Goddamnit," he said, "just tell them we got an operation with Americans on it in heavy contact and that we need air cover. Tell 'em I'm busy. Tell them to stand by!" and he resumed trying to talk to one of the LLDB members. I went back to our commo bunker mumbling to myself and relayed the message to Cross.

"They ain't gonna like it," Cross said as he began operating the Morse code key. We were receiving over a speaker, and I heard the B-detachment radio operator at the other end acknowledge the message and send the Morse code signal to "wait." Then, almost immediately, there came the reply from higher headquarters: *This is the B-detachment commander. I want your detachment commander standing by to give me exact situation. Now.*

"This is gonna be a long day," I told Cross as I went to look for Arsenault.

More dead and wounded were arriving all the time, and the full extent of the developing battle was becoming apparent. As yet, none of the American or Vietnamese Special Forces had made it back, and we were getting very worried. We interrogated each returning group of defeated CIDG about our teammates but got many conflicting reports. Some told us they had been killed already, some said they were captured, and some claimed they were all still fighting valiantly on. From what we could gather, the operation had run into an enemy force of at least battalion size, probably larger.

By early afternoon we knew we were in deep trouble and sent our first message requesting that a reaction force be helicoptered in for reinforcement. The B-detachment commander still demanded that Arsenault stand by the radio to send him updates, and, of course, our detachment CO had many more pressing matters to attend to. Higher headquarters had never really believed any of the frequent intelligence reports we'd sent them concerning the strength of the enemy around Tan Phu, and now they were reluctant to believe that our situation was as serious as we were telling them.

Evidently the CV-2 and its armed escort had reported receiving ground fire, and at about 1400 hours two armed T-28s arrived overhead with an L-19 "bird dog" spotter. They were unable to contact any friendly forces in the battle area and could not distinguish good guys from bad guys. They continued to circle the area all afternoon looking for a confirmed target of opportunity.

Sergeant VandeBerg, our team's junior medic, had his hands full. Although he and Pitzer, our medical supervisor, had done a good job of training two or three Vietnamese women as nurses, and although the LLDB medic was also fairly well trained, the magnitude of the situation strained his resources. He was dealing with everything from blown-off arms and legs, sucking chest wounds, and massive head injuries, to ripped-open stomachs and emasculations.

In these early days of the war there were few helicopters in-country. Although we Americans could count on fairly speedy evacuation by helicopter to the Eighth Field Hospital in Nha Trang, our Vietnamese troops had to depend on the limited Vietnamese air and medical resources. Since our CIDG forces had lowest priority for all types of support, they were mainly dependent on what medical treatment they could get from the U.S. Special Forces medics.

A GP-medium tent was hastily erected next to the camp dispensary to act as the morgue. It quickly filled up as the bodies were stacked like cordwood on the ground inside. Many of the dead and wounded had family members in the nearby village. As these wives and children started arriving, they added to the confusion with their wails of grief and sorrow.

Sidney Cross was the only black guy on our team, and I'm sure he always felt a little lonely. In the last couple of months Sidney had become quite close to one of our Cambodian troops whose skin was almost as dark as his. Sidney spent many hours in the evenings teaching the young Cambodian English. On one of my frequent trips that day trying to corral Arsenault and bring him back to the commo bunker, I found my fellow radio operator in the makeshift morgue looking down at the mangled body of his friend, the Cambodian. There were tears in Sidney's eyes as he mourned his loss.

The LLDB commander, Lieutenant Tinh, their team sergeant, Canh, and their radio operator, Dih Dah, finally made it back to camp from the operation. Tinh and Dih Dah were both wounded, and Tinh told us the situation was as bad as we feared. They had no new information on the condition of the Americans, nor of their LLDB intel sergeant, Pee Hole, who was also MIA. "Beaucoup VC," Lieutenant Tinh said over and over again, "beaucoup VC."

We knew we had to try to send some sort of relief force to the battle area, but we also knew the Viet Cong would be lying in wait for them. Pinning down one unit and then ambushing the rescuers was a very old guerrilla tactic that the communists had been successfully using since their war with the French. Besides that, we didn't have many troops left to draw from. Other than the untrained, unarmed Cambodian company, we had only one combat-ready company still in camp. The few survivors who had managed to make it back from the operation were too shattered to go out again.

There was a hurried meeting with the LLDB team and the decision was made to arm the Cambodians, use them only for camp defense, and attempt to send our remaining able-bodied troops into the fray. Although all members of our detachment volunteered to accompany this risky operation, the sad fact was that we could risk no more U.S. personnel. Sergeant Canh was an old, experienced soldier, and he bravely volunteered to accompany the relief force along with two other LLDB members.

Martin and our combat engineer sergeant, Carey, immediately went to work issuing arms and ammunition to the Cambodians. As the Cambodians took up defensive positions on the camp perimeter, they relieved members of Second Company, who prepared themselves for action. Second Company knew they would be walking into a real shitstorm, and they lacked their usual high morale and bravado.

The U.S. team members watched Second Company move off toward the battle area with mixed emotions. On one hand, we hoped the relief force would be successful and bring back our comrades. On the other, we had only a few hours until dark, and we were left in camp with only a few wounded and demoralized survivors and one company of untrained troops whose loyalty we were uncertain of.

As it turned out, Second Company hit a VC blocking force within two kilometers of our camp. Heavy fighting

ensued and we took more casualties. We'd still received
no word from higher headquarters concerning our
requested reinforcements and had given up hope of getting any outside help until the next morning—if we survived until then. We ordered Second Company to break
contact and return to camp.

The troops of Second Company had fired up most of
their ammunition and had to be resupplied. More dead
and wounded arrived every minute. Tan Phu was at the
intersection of two canals, one of which flowed in our
direction from the battle area, and bodies of both friendly
and enemy troops began to float past in the water. We
had only an hour until dark, when I received the terse
coded message from the B-team that choppers were on
the way with help.

Martin and I were given the job of securing the landing
zone for the incoming reaction force. They were late in
arriving, and Bill and I were feeling more and more
exposed and vulnerable as we crouched in knee-deep
water behind a dike in the open rice paddy. We had only
a platoon with us, whom we had deployed in a loose
perimeter, most of them defending a nearby tree line that
would be the most likely direction of an attack. Dusk had
fallen, and we carried flashlights to guide the chopper
pilots in.

The T-28s were still circling over the area, but the
L-19 had run low on fuel and returned to Camau. We'd
just heard the distinctive sound of the incoming Huey's
rotors when Bill yelled, "Holy shit, get down!"

Along the canal bank, less than a kilometer away,
seven streams of bright tracers suddenly arched up in the
twilight toward one of the T-28s. Bill and I stood up
again, embarrassed, and laughed shakily. For a split

second we'd thought the fire was directed our way. The T-28s each made one strafing run at the enemy machine guns, then flew off in the gathering darkness toward Saigon.

The chopper pilots had seen the enemy firepower display and wasted no time in dropping off their load of troops and clearing the area. The reaction force was a full company of CIA-trained Vietnamese Special Forces. Working directly under President Diem's brother, Nhu, they were part of his Palace Guard and were some of the best Vietnamese troops available at the time. They looked impressively professional as they quickly deployed and moved smartly off the LZ and into our camp. Of course, the way we felt by then, a troop of Boy Scouts would have been welcome.

Chapter 2

After my graduation from Special Forces Training Group at Fort Bragg in November of 1962, there were four Special Forces units I might have been assigned to. The old 77th Group had been renamed the 7th and was located a few blocks up the street from Training Group on Smoke Bomb Hill. The 7th Group's area of responsibility was Latin America, and they had many Spanish-speaking members.

The 10th Group was in Germany at Bad Tolz. The 10th ran missions throughout all of Europe, had a hush-hush detachment in Berlin, and was where most of the new Training Group graduates wanted to go. The 1st Special Forces was stationed on Okinawa, operated in various countries of Asia, and was known to be performing many missions in Laos and Vietnam.

A new Group, the 5th, had recently been activated, and was located just at the bottom of Smoke Bomb. The 5th was still at about half strength and consisted of only a headquarters and two companies. It had no known strategic area of interest and was believed to be getting stuck pulling a lot of "ash-'n'-trash" details around Fort Bragg. No one, including me, wanted to get assigned there.

Where I wanted to go was where all the combat action was—the 1st SF on Okinawa. I bribed one of the clerks at Training Group headquarters with a bottle of whiskey to make sure I was placed on the levy to the 1st Group, sat back confidently with dreams of exotic, tropical lands in mind, and awaited my orders.

A week later my assignment finally came. I disgustedly jammed everything I owned in my duffel bag, hoisted it on my shoulder, and made the short walk down the hill to my new home, Company B, 5th Special Forces. Once there, I learned some good news and some bad news. The good news was that the 5th was actually sending a few A-teams on six-month, temporary-duty missions to Vietnam. The bad news was that it was difficult to get on one of these teams, and because I was one of five men in the whole 5th Group below the rank of sergeant, I could expect to be pulling a lot of KP and guard duty.

The 7th, 5th, and Training Groups were billeted in the old-style, two-story wooden barracks. These buildings had been refurbished somewhat and were livable, but were still a long cry from the newer concrete barracks then being built. If you were enlisted, single, and below the rank of sergeant first class, you lived in an open bay in the barracks. You became one of the "barracks rats," as opposed to that other, luckier group, known as "shack rats."

In the early sixties the Army still didn't get paid very much. We usually worked a five-and-a-half-day week, the half day being the hated, Saturday-morning barracks and equipment inspection. Most junior-grade enlisted soldiers couldn't afford automobiles, so we had to depend either on the shuttle bus or on the one or two other guys who did have cars. The social life available for us enlisted swine hadn't changed dramatically since the time of the Roman Legions. The three main off-duty occupations were: drinking, gambling, and trying to get laid.

Drinking was the easiest of the three to do and was interwoven in the very fabric of Army life. There was a thriving club system on post that sold discount-price booze and frequently offered live entertainment. There was a thriving clip-joint system outside every post gate that offered overpriced drinks. Occasionally there would be company parties that featured all the booze you could drink for free.

No one in leadership cared how much a soldier drank on his off time so long as he was "standing tall" at the reveille formation the next morning and was able to do his assigned job. Getting drunk on duty was not accepted behavior, but no one particularly cared if an NCO ate lunch at his club and downed a couple of beers. The popular motto was: "We work hard together and play hard together."

Keeping alcohol, or getting drunk in the barracks itself, was against the rules, and for the most part we barracks rats obeyed. Why run the risk of hiding a bottle in your footlocker when there was a club within walking distance? Gambling in the barracks was also against the rules, but no one bothered to enforce it. For the most part, the gambling involved various nickel-dime card games and no one ever got hurt too much. Different card games came in and out of vogue, the biggest ones being poker, pitch, and rummy.

The main thing on the minds of us impoverished, single, young barracks rats was *sex*. Of the big-three pastimes, this was the most difficult one to come by, particularly when stationed in the U.S. The ratio of available men to women around any Army post was always about one thousand to one. For the most part, local girls wouldn't have anything to do with a soldier. This was before the so-called Sexual Revolution, and "good girls" didn't go out with GIs.

There were always a few prostitutes working the dives around Fort Bragg and other posts, but in the U.S. these were overpriced, elderly, ugly, and oftentimes diseased. The older NCOs had it a little better, because there were generally some local "sweat hogs" who hung around the NCO clubs looking for some action. Women didn't come to the EM clubs, though.

The situation was always much better for those stationed overseas, and this was one of the main inducements for a soldier to seek assignment to Europe or Asia. The girls overseas had a more enlightened attitude toward American troops than did the women back home. Prostitution was an accepted and sometimes legal occupation in many foreign countries, and the girls selling it there were younger, prettier, nicer, and more affordable. In a country like Vietnam you had all of this plus the chance to get involved with a real shooting war. Hell, no wonder we were so anxious to get over there!

The commander of the 5th Group at this time was an imposing full colonel by the name of "Chill" Wills. Wills was an old paratroop officer who was a combat veteran of every war in recent memory. He was a strict disciplinarian who really cracked the whip, and most of us, especially the young officers, were terrified of him.

We had a long, four-day weekend coming up that Christmas of 1962; it was Friday afternoon and everyone was anxious to get it started. We could see guys from the 7th Group and even from the 82nd Airborne already driving down Smoke Bomb on their way home, but we still hadn't been released. Suddenly we received word to fall out on the parade field for a group formation.

Grumbling and cursing under our breaths, we formed up and then had to stand around for fifteen minutes waiting for Wills to arrive. All this time we had to put up with the laughter, jeers, waves, and honks of the guys from the other units as they gaily drove past on their way off post. We supposed this was all so Wills could give us the usual "have a nice, but safe holiday" speech.

Wills finally came striding to the podium from his headquarters building and immediately launched into a harangue that was to become a classic. He was not happy about all the tickets we'd been getting for driving under the influence, he told us. As a result, he was having concertina wire strung around part of the 5th Group parking lot. From then on, he said, talking louder and louder and becoming more and more inflamed, anyone in *his* unit who received a DWI would park their cars in the new impoundment lot, put it up on blocks, and be required to walk guard duty around it at night. The punishment period for first offense was thirty days, and if you had a second offense, God help you!

By this time he was fully warmed up, yelling, and practically frothing at the mouth. "I don't care what your goddamned rank is, whether you're a lieutenant colonel, sergeant major, or recruit. I don't care if you're driving a truck, a car, a motorcycle, a bicycle, or a fucking *tricycle*—if you get a DWI, you'll put it on blocks! And if you don't believe me," he continued, glaring at us with eyes that seemed to bug out of his head, "just try me . . . just fucking try me. Now, are there any stupid questions?" Of course, there were none. "Okay, I guess we understand each other," he said, finally quieting down a little. "Have a merry fucking Christmas," he concluded with a growl, then spun on his heel and marched back to his headquarters.

Shortly after the Christmas holiday, to get off the KP roster, I volunteered to be a fireman. This was the kind of fireman who shovels coal into heating furnaces, not the kind that puts out fires. I kept the fires burning in the day room and the orderly room on a twenty-four-hour on, twenty-four-hour off shift and tried to keep a good attitude. Shoveling coal is a dirty, filthy job, and firemen were noted for their slovenly appearance. I'd learned how to soldier in the 101st Airborne, though, and I decided to be the sharpest-looking fireman in Special Forces.

One cold morning near the end of my shift, I was approached by a snotty second lieutenant who was pulling staff duty in the orderly room. He told me, in a rather surly manner, that the orderly room was not warm enough, that the commander and his staff would be there shortly, and that I should immediately get my lazy ass over and get the fire going better. My good attitude slipped a notch or two.

"Hot? You want it *hot*?" I mumbled to myself as I opened all the dampers and threw more coal in the already blazing furnace. "How's this, shithead?" Then, with the furnace walls beginning to glow dark red, I went back to the barracks and lay on my bunk.

An hour or so later an apologetic sergeant major found me. "Ah, could you come over and do something about the heat?" he asked. "The blowers won't shut off. We have all the windows open, but it's so hot in there that the paint is peeling off the walls and the fluorescent lights keep blinking on and off!"

I took care of the problem for him, and I believe that's how I came to the attention of the powers that be in the orderly room. A few days later the sergeant major told me that they had an open slot for a radio operator on a "go" team, and he asked me if I wanted to go to Vietnam. I don't think I actually dropped down and kissed his feet, but that was how I felt. Later that day I moved my stuff upstairs in the barracks and met the other members of A-23, my new detachment.

Captain Bob Leites was the detachment commander. Leites was an ex–master sergeant, a Korean War veteran, and a very experienced soldier. Leites was known as "Mr. Clean" due to his completely bald head and stocky build. He told me he was glad to have me because I was filling the last vacant slot on the team, and they were now fully up to TO&E strength.

A young West Pointer, Lieutenant James "Nick" Rowe, was the detachment executive officer. Lieutenant Rowe's style of friendly, low-key leadership was a perfect complement to Captain Leites's gruff, ex-first-sergeant style. West Point officers were a rarity in Special Forces in those days, and in fact Rowe was the first one I had yet served under in my short Army career. Lieutenant Rowe was an artillery officer, had been through the Special Forces officer training program, and had recently graduated from the Chinese-language course at the Defense Language Institute in Monterey.

Our team sergeant was Tom Kemmer. Master Sergeant Kemmer was another old hand and worked well with both Leites and Rowe. Master Sergeant Kemmer was a graduate of the Navy UDT school, among other exotic qualifications, and was well-connected with the "Senior NCO Mafia," which, I'd discovered, really ran things in Special Forces units.

Sergeant First Class Norman Hardy was the other operations and intelligence specialist on the team and filled the slot of intelligence sergeant. Norm was a quiet, friendly man who was devoted to his family and church. Our two weapons NCOs were John Lowe and Ponce Navarro. "Big John" was one of those country-boy types and a real expert with the 81mm mortar. Ponce was a Hawaiian soldier from the old school. Navarro had just returned from a tour in Vietnam and was the only one on our detachment with prior experience of the country. Although Ponce was filling the slot of light weapons NCO, he also was a trained radio operator.

Filling the medical positions were SFC Dan Pitzer and Sgt. Roger VandeBerg. Dan was a veteran of the Korean War and was another of our NCOs who had a lot of prior Army experience under his belt. VandeBerg had given "four to the Corps" before seeing the light, getting out of the Marines, and joining the Army. Roger, I soon discovered, went by the nickname "Warthog," a name he had earned not by his looks, but by the horrible way he snored at night.

The position of "demolitions sergeant" on Special Forces A-teams had recently been expanded in scope and training to become "engineer sergeant." Our senior engineer sergeant, S.Sgt. Ken Carey, had just returned from the bridge and construction course at Fort Belvoir. Carey's assistant was a tall, lanky guy from Texas, PFC Bill Martin. Although Bill had more time in the Army than I did, he was the only one on the team whom I outranked.

Bill had celebrated his promotion to Specialist Fourth Class about a year earlier by getting drunk, stealing a Military Police jeep, and leading the furious MPs on a wild chase around Fort Bragg. He finally went in a ditch and was captured. In today's Army he would have been jailed or at least summarily discharged for such an offense. In those days, however, it wasn't such a big deal. It had only been an MP jeep, after all. It had taken place within the confines of the military reservation, and Bill was an otherwise excellent soldier. His punishment for the offense had been reduction in rank back to private, and restriction to the company area for a few weeks. At the time I met him, Bill was busy soldiering his way back up through the ranks.

The detachment senior radio operator, whom I would be working most closely with, was another young guy about my age named Sidney Cross. Being black, Sidney was not only a rarity on our team, but at that time was one of the few black soldiers in Special Forces. Although the military had been integrated for some time, segregation in the civilian sector was still pretty much in full swing, especially in the southern states. Sidney and I became good friends, and he was completely accepted by the other detachment members as part of the team. It was rather sad, however, that although we could all party and drink together while still on the military reservation of Fort Bragg, once we left the front gate, Sidney went his way and we went ours.

The barracks rats from three "go" teams, A-21, A-22, and A-23, lived together in an open bay on the top floor. We trained together all day and partied together all night. The medic on detachment A-21 was a young buck sergeant by the name of Smith. Smith had the only

car among us, a huge, rusted-out Edsel that we affection-
ately called the Big E. The Big E had bald tires, no
shocks, no brakes, the lights didn't always work, and the
heater and air conditioner were broken. But, boy, would
that baby fly, especially after a night of hitting the beer
joints!

Soon after I was assigned to A-23, the three Vietnam-
bound A-detachments started a premission training
cycle. Although some of the older guys thought this was
mainly wasted time, I enjoyed the training and got a lot
out of it. The first four hours in the mornings were spent
in language training. Half the team studied Vietnamese
and the others studied French. I was in the group that
took French, and since I had already studied the language
in high school, it was mostly a refresher course for me.

Most afternoons we cross-trained in the various team
specialties. We attended many lectures on such things as
the religion, economics, and politics of Vietnam. Some
days we went to the demo or weapons ranges, or did
something more physical like hand-to-hand combat
training or long marches with full rucksacks. Parachute
operations, some performed with the Air Force's newly
activated Air Commandos, were frequent.

There was a recommended reading list, and some of
the popular books making the rounds in those days were
things such as *The Quiet American*, by Greene, *The Cen-
turions*, by Larteguy, and *Street Without Joy*, by Fall. We
also read the works on guerrilla warfare by Mao and
T. E. Lawrence. Kipling was the poet of choice. Special
Forces always had a smarter, better-educated bunch of
men than the average Army unit, and many of us had lit-
erary interests. Of course, we didn't let all this reading
interfere with our nightly drinking and carousing!

We trained hard that spring of '63 and culminated it with a two-week field-training exercise that attempted to simulate the various situations we might soon face in Vietnam. The exercise ended with a scenario during which our "CIDG camp" was overrun, causing us to go into an escape and evasion mode. Our E&E lasted several days and was quite strenuous, but we finally made it back to "friendly territory." As soon as we cleaned all our equipment, turned it in, and attended a debriefing on our training efforts, we were released to go on a two-week, predeployment furlough.

I went back to Tucson, Arizona, and visited my mother and father. It was the first time I'd been back in almost two years, and it was good to see them and my old school friends again. It was pretty obvious, however, that a large gulf had developed between my old school chums and me. They had all stayed in Tucson after I'd departed for the Army, and most of them were going to the University of Arizona. They were still dating the same old girls, doing the same things, and going to the same places they'd been going to when we were in high school. None of them had ever even heard of a country named Vietnam. Besides, they were all civilians.

It was actually good to get back to Fort Bragg, my bunk, wall lockers and footlockers, and the other guys in the barracks. It was like coming home again after an interesting but exhausting vacation. I had developed into a professional soldier, a lifer, and hadn't even noticed.

Chapter 3

We left Pope airfield in a KC-135 on July 10, 1963. A KC-135 was an Air Force tanker that had been converted to carry passengers. All the seats faced backward, an aid to safety in case of a crash, and there were only two small windows in the cabin. Although we had four A-teams on the plane and all our equipment, there was still plenty of room. As soon as we got airborne and could unbuckle our seat belts, some of our card players found an open area on the floor in the rear of the plane and began a game.

The flight plan called for us to fly nonstop from Pope airfield to Hawaii, refuel, then fly on directly to Tan Son Nhut in Saigon. As luck would have it, however, our pilot was an old Air Force colonel who was mixing a little business with pleasure. When we landed at Honolulu, the crew chief told us with mock dismay that instead of only a two-hour layover, it looked like we would be staying there "at least a day or two." Mysterious mechanical difficulties had developed and needed to be repaired before we continued on, he told us with a wink.

"Just check back with flight operations in about twenty-four hours," the pilot said, loading his golf clubs into a waiting staff car. "We'll kind of play it by ear." I was beginning to really like the Air Force.

Our detachment decided not to even attempt to find lodgings, but to party the entire time we were on the island. We divided into two groups, piled into rental cars, and headed for Honolulu.

We actually got some sight-seeing done first. Navarro was with our group, and he acted as a tour guide as he showed us his hometown. We saw all the usual attractions and even took a drive around to the north side of the island on Highway 83. When night fell, we dropped the tourist bit and got down to some serious debauchery. After twenty-four hours of nonstop revelry, we found out the Air Force would need another twelve hours for more "maintenance." By the time we finally climbed back aboard to continue, we were some sick dudes, believe me.

It didn't end there, either. The crew chief came back and told us that because of all the mechanical problems we'd been having, the pilot had decided we would also have to land on Okinawa before completing our trip. This really thrilled me, because the many ex-members of 1st Group with us started telling us about all the great bars, clubs, whorehouses, and massage parlors that awaited us there.

We landed at Kadena Air Base in the late afternoon and were informed that this layover would be for only twelve hours. We were taken by bus to temporary quarters behind the Camp Kue hospital, warned to be back not later than 0400 hours because takeoff time was 0600, then turned loose. Many of the guys were too exhausted from our stop in Honolulu to do anything except collapse on their cots and sleep. Most of us younger guys, driven on by raging hormones, jumped in taxis and headed for the fleshpots of B.C. and Gate Two streets in Kadena.

I had a few drinks at the bars on Gate Two, then cut through Whisper Alley to B.C. From darkened doorways came the leering, whispered invitations that gave the short alley its name. "Hey, GI, you want blow job? Only one dollar!"

I made it through this obstacle course with my virtue still intact and went into a bar called the Ace of Clubs. Once there, I was immediately and expertly taken over by a cute little barmaid who wanted me to buy her drinks all evening. She was drinking real booze and she could really belt 'em down. When the joint closed at midnight, I accompanied her to her one-room home, which she shared with a twelve-year-old sister and one-year-old daughter.

Once under the harsher light of her room, I discovered that she was maybe not as young as I had previously thought. The fact that we had to perform our hurried sex act with her sister tending the crying baby five feet away on the other side of a curtain also tended to ruin the romantic atmosphere somewhat . . . but not that much.

I dozed off and just by pure luck woke up and glanced at my watch. It was already 0345 hours, fifteen minutes until I had to be back at the barracks! I leaped up and frantically started dressing.

"Must go, must go," I told her, breaking into that pidgin English that Americans think they must use with foreigners. "You, taxi-me. Go Kue. *Muy pronto, vite-vite!*"

"Speak English, please. Are you saying you want a taxi so you can go to Camp Kue?" she said calmly from where she still lay on the futon. I think I detected a faint smile on her otherwise impassive face.

When I drove up to the barracks at Kue, all the lights were blazing, the bus was out front, and men were already loading baggage into it. I leaped from the taxi just in time to hear Kemmer yelling to someone inside, "Where the fuck is Wade? Has anyone seen him?" I ran in, ripped off my civilian clothes, and boarded the bus as it left for the airfield. I was still lacing up my boots when Kemmer glanced over at me from his seat across the aisle. "Cutting it a little close, weren't you?" he said, obviously not too happy with me. It had been a near thing, but worth it!

We landed at Tan Son Nhut in the morning of one of those hot, humid days that we would soon become very accustomed to. The men of the four new A-teams got off the plane and watched as our pallets of equipment were unloaded. I was a little nervous as I looked around, half expecting a squad of commie infiltrators to come bursting out of nowhere at any moment, guns blazing. In actuality, although there were a few Vietnamese and American soldiers walking around, there was little outward sign that there was a war going on. We had landed right in front of the large, glass-walled civilian air terminal, and it was filled with civilian travelers going about their normal routines.

There were men from several teams who had just completed their six-month tours standing around. They were waiting to get on the C-135 we had just arrived in for the return trip to Bragg. We were the "newbies" and they were the "old Asia hands," and I looked at them for any visible signs of what they'd been through in the last six months.

The main difference between their group and ours was that they were much more subdued and quiet than we were. I'd have thought they would have been more boisterous and happy to be leaving. They were all very thin, deeply tanned, and their jungle fatigue uniforms were bleached and ragged looking. I didn't know any of them, but some of our bunch recognized old friends and went over to say hello. I was half expecting them all to give us a chorus of "You'll be sorryyyyy!" as they boarded the C-135, but I guess they just weren't in the mood.

We were supposed to transfer to C-123s for the ride to the Special Forces headquarters up in Nha Trang, but of course the planes weren't there yet. We sat around for a while in the meager patches of shade we could find on the broiling hot tarmac, then someone made the command decision that we could just as well all wait in the civilian air terminal.

The terminal was cool inside, filled with pretty girls of various nationalities, and had a bar on the upper level. There was a place to change dollars into piasters, and once armed with the proper currency, we retired to the lounge. Sitting there sipping an ice-cold "33" beer, checking out the beautiful Vietnamese bartender in her pink and white *au dai*, I decided that so far this warfighting stuff had been pretty fun.

Eventually two C-123s arrived and we had to go back to work breaking down our team equipment from the pallets and hand-loading it aboard the smaller aircraft. These planes were flown by Air Commando crews, an outfit we all enjoyed working with. Our pilot was dressed in a flight suit with no sleeves, had his bush hat pulled low over his eyes, and wore elephant-hide cowboy boots. He gave us a typical, Air Commando preflight briefing.

"Wellll," he drawled, taking the toothpick out of his mouth, "the crew chief tells me that we're a little overloaded." He flipped the toothpick away. "We got a long runway here at Son Nhut and we got these here JATO bottles on the wings, so we're gonna give it a try anyway." He took off his bush hat and adjusted the peacock feather stuck under the hatband. "As soon as we get airborne I'll lower the tailgate to get some air circulating. It might be a little bumpy in this hot air," he added as an afterthought, "make sure no one falls out, heh-heh."

We used up every bit of the runway on our takeoff, and the roar of the jets as they cut in at what seemed to be the last possible moment was deafening, but once we got airborne, the ride was actually quite pleasant. We had a great view of the countryside out of the open tailgate. I was overwhelmed by the beauty of the landscape, and I suddenly had what was practically a mystical experience. *This is what you were born to do and this is where you will do it,* an inner voice whispered.

We circled Nha Trang a couple of times before landing and got a good view of the beautiful, unspoiled beach and surrounding terrain. If I'd taken a picture, I could have sold it to a travel agency. Our plane bumped down on the runway, which was at that time still simply dirt covered with pierced steel planking. We taxied to a parking area at the end of the strip, the pilot cut the engines, and we got out. After a short wait a couple of $2^1/_2$-ton trucks driven by Vietnamese and a jeep carrying two Americans roared up. The Americans were dressed in shorts, Hawaiian shirts, and flip-flops.

They introduced themselves as representatives of the C-detachment. "We been looking for you for two days," one of them said. "Sorry about the civilian clothes, but we've already knocked off work for the day. Throw your stuff in the trucks and follow us, we'll take you to your billets, then show you our new club!"

The Special Forces headquarters complex in 1963 consisted of buildings with waist-high concrete-block walls, screen the rest of the way up, and palm thatch roofs. They had just built their club and were very proud of it. It was decorated in early "Terry and the Pirates" motif with touches of Indochinese whorehouse/opium den. Ceiling fans circulated the hot, heavy air. There was lots of rattan furniture, beaded curtains, and bamboo. Two pretty Vietnamese girls tended the well-stocked bar. We had a great night with the guys at the C-team, and the next morning began our in-processing.

We began the day by drawing weapons and going to the local range to test-fire and sight them in. The standard-issue weapon for Special Forces in Vietnam in 1963 was the WWII-vintage M-2 carbine. Many of us didn't particularly like the carbine, but we were told that once we got to our CIDG camps, we would have our pick of a much wider selection of firearms.

Next, we attended briefings on the general situation in-country at that time and on the role Special Forces was playing. Up until then, Special Forces in Vietnam had worked for the CIA, but now we found out that something called Operation Switchback had started and we would be reverting back to Army control. None of us were very glad to hear this, frankly, because life was always much better for us when we worked for the "Agency."

The Strategic Hamlet, or Civilian Irregular Defense Group program, was a CIA idea. The original plan was to move Special Forces teams into many little towns and villages where the VC threat was not too great, establish minimal defensive positions, arm and train some of the local young men to defend themselves against VC bullies, and then perform civic action projects to improve life out in the rural areas.

The CIA version of this program was strictly defensive. Most of the armed civilians were supposed to be only part-time soldiers, happily working their rice fields, but with their guns nearby just in case. A small group called a strike force would be better trained and better armed and would be the only full-time soldiers. The CIA had actually stolen this idea from the British, who had successfully used it against communist insurgents in Malaya.

There were several problems with this scheme. First of all, in many of the areas where these Strategic Hamlets were initiated, the VC weren't just a few roving bands of bullies, but hardcore, well-armed, skillfully led units of up to battalion size. The other problem was that Special Forces figured that the best defense is a good offense. It was suicidal to stay strictly on the defensive, as the CIA had originally envisioned it. The small strike forces grew larger and larger, began running offensive operations farther and farther away from the camps, and eventually became the main focus of the CIDG program.

By that summer of '63, some of the CIDG camps were in fairly safe areas and were still operating pretty much as the CIA had originally planned. Some camps were in hotter areas and had strike forces of battalion size. None of these camps were really very secure, and the regular American and Vietnamese army expected them to all be overrun sooner or later. For this reason, there were many restrictions on the types of arms and ammunition the CIDG units could have.

That afternoon, we split up into specialty areas, and Cross and I got our commo briefing. Communication between the deployed teams and higher headquarters was really quite simple. The C-team in Nha Trang operated a radio net between themselves and four B-teams, one of which was located in each corps area. Each B-team had four or five A-teams under it and operated one net between the deployed teams and another net with the C-team. The C-team and B-teams monitored their nets twenty-four hours a day, but the A-teams made only several scheduled contacts each day. All communications were in Morse code. Most traffic was sent encrypted, using what is known as a "one-time pad." At the tactical level, the A-teams and their strike forces used voice radios.

That evening we had a team meeting and passed around all the information we had received. Captain Leites had the most exciting news: our team was being sent down to a place named Tan Phu in the Mekong Delta. It was considered one of the most dangerous CIDG camps in Vietnam, with plenty of VC activity. We were all glad to get this assignment. Soon we would "get a little action and start kicking some ass," as someone on the team remarked.

The next morning we would fly down to the B-team in Can Tho. I slept like a log that night. I didn't know it at the time, but this was the last good night's sleep I was to have for the next six months.

Chapter 4

The B-team headquarters at Can Tho was on the edge of town next to the airfield. It had been built in a square with an open area in the center and a concrete machine-gun emplacement on each corner. It followed the usual design of a waist-high block wall with screens up to a palm thatch roof. The B-team communications and operations occupied one side of the square, the mess hall was in another, and the remainder of the building consisted of sleeping quarters and, of course, a club. The place looked like it was designed for a last stand, and for this reason it was nicknamed "the Alamo."

There was much more evidence that there was an actual war going on around Can Tho, and the Alamo didn't look all that damned secure. We were immediately assured that Can Tho was a "pacified area" and that nothing ever happened around there. I talked to some of the B-team radio operators who were finishing their tours, and they said they hadn't heard a shot fired in all the six months they'd been there.

All of us were worn out by this time, and the next morning we'd be taken by helicopter to our camps. After a couple of beers in the club, we turned in early. Our sister team, A-21, had also been assigned to a camp in the Delta named Hiep Hoa, and representatives from that team and from Tan Phu had come to the B-team to brief us. This made for very crowded conditions in our sleeping quarters. I flopped down on the folding canvas cot, adjusted the mosquito net around me, and zonked out.

Blamm! I jerked awake. At first I thought it was the nearby battery of 155 howitzers firing a little interdiction.

Kerboom-wham-bang!! Snap-pop-crack . . . Slugs ripped through the wire screen over my head. Holy shit, I thought, automatically rolling off my cot to the hard cement floor, that's *incoming*!

One of the corner machine guns opened up, and it sounded like the gunner fired off the entire 250-round belt in a single burst. "Get to the outer walls!" someone yelled. "Get your weapons and get a firing position!"

"They're coming through the front gate!" another voice outside yelled, sending chills up my spine.

I was just peering over the edge of the block wall trying to find something to shoot at when there was a flash and a deafening crash almost directly over my head. This was followed by a brief moment of what seemed like utter silence, then all around me men started yelling, moaning, and cursing.

"Medic! Medic! . . . Jesus, what-the-fuck . . . Shit, I'm hit . . ." One of the team sergeants was yelling for his team medic to get his aid bag. "I can't, Sarge," came the reply, "I got a slug in me!" The crowded room was filled with the acrid smell of burnt powder.

Just as suddenly as it started, all the firing now ended. I wasn't hit, and I crawled over to the doorway wondering what had happened to the enemy horde who were supposedly coming through the front gate. There were no enemy, only dazed American Special Forces troops running every which way.

A single 60mm mortar round had made a direct hit on the roof of the sleeping quarters. It had passed through the thatch without detonating, then struck a cross beam and exploded with devastating effect. The airburst had wounded fourteen men, a couple of them seriously.

Kemmer was one of the worst hit. He'd taken a large piece of frag through the wrist. Martin had assorted holes in his head, shoulder, and back. Cross was hit in the thigh, and Pitzer had a couple of wounds. Lowe had the most embarrassing wound: a large hunk of shrapnel had got him right in the ass. "Felt like someone slapped me on the butt with a big ol' board," is how he sheepishly explained it.

There was a hospital in the town of Can Tho, and the wounded were taken there for immediate attention. The ride from the Alamo to the hospital was made in two jeeps at breakneck speed, and several guys told me that this trip was much more terrifying than the attack. In the meantime the rest of us took up fighting positions around the outer walls in case of another attack.

I spent the remainder of the night in the corner machine-gun position that had been doing so much shooting. I listened to war stories from the two excited CIDG gunners as the three of us smoked up all my American cigarettes and then started on their Vietnamese brand, Ruby Queen. They told me of being able to see the flashes of the enemy small arms and mortars and of returning fire with great gusto. The number of enemy they killed steadily grew as the night dragged on. I was glad when the sun came up and the danger of another attack was over. We had no spare barrel for the .30

machine gun, and I figured the one in it was probably melted.

Later that morning we had a briefing on the night's activity and were told that the main attack had been directed against the airfield. The rounds fired in our direction were only to keep us pinned down, and the mortar hit on the roof was just luck on the enemy's part.

I didn't believe this version of the story then and I don't believe it now. I think the attack was primarily against us and was done to welcome us to the Delta. I believe it was the beginning of a general offensive by the VC against the ever-growing Special Forces and CIDG presence in Vietnam.

Our wounded were evacuated to the Eighth Field Army Hospital in Nha Trang. We didn't know at the time when or if any of these men would be returning to the team. We basically had a half detachment remaining with at least one man in each specialty area, so we could still relieve the waiting team at Tan Phu as scheduled.

Chapter 5

Tan Phu was on the edge of the U Minh forest, which had been a Viet Cong stronghold for many years. The camp lay at the intersection of two major canals and next to an abandoned dirt road the French had built. Our mission was to control traffic on the waterways, secure the immediate area to allow the road to be reopened, perform civic action in the nearby village, and kill Viet Cong.

The team we were relieving, A-20, had opened the camp after a large unit of regular Vietnamese infantry performed extensive clearing operations. The outgoing team had been there for three months and construction of living quarters and initial defensive positions had been completed. They had so far recruited, trained, and armed two CIDG companies of one hundred men each. We would need to recruit at least two more companies to perform the type of aggressive offensive operations that were expected of us.

It was possible to get into Tan Phu only by helicopter or parachute, and the seven unwounded members of our team arrived in the early afternoon via H-21. We had only two days with the old team before they left us on our own, and we immediately got down to work. The first order of business was meeting our Vietnamese Special Forces counterparts.

In 1963 the quality of Vietnamese Special Forces, or Luc Luong Dac Biet (LLDB), varied from absolutely worthless to very good. The LLDB were under direct control of Diem's brother, Nhu. Many of the LLDB were purely political appointments with no military training or experience. Some, however, were old soldiers. Many had attended special training conducted by the CIA and American Special Forces.

Major Phong, the LLDB detachment commander at Tan Phu, was both an old, experienced soldier and a politically connected one. Phong had originally started his military career fighting with the Viet Minh against the French. Because Phong was Catholic and anticommunist, he'd moved south and joined Diem once the French had been beaten. During his Viet Minh days Phong had actually fought alongside several of the Viet Cong commanders we faced at Tan Phu. Phong had a wealth of information concerning VC tactics and potentials, but he was also a survivor and interested in advancing his own career. He was fluent in both English and French, had a beautiful wife and two teenage daughters in Saigon, and found many excuses to leave camp for trips to higher headquarters.

Lieutenant Tinh was Phong's executive officer. Tinh was a quiet, personable young officer with little experience, but was a man who tried to do a good job. Because Phong was a powerful commander, Tinh had little to do. Sergeant Canh was the LLDB team sergeant, another old, experienced soldier. Although Canh had fought with a French parachute unit against the Viet Minh, he and Phong seemed to get along just fine.

We were also introduced to the LLDB intelligence sergeant, who had picked up the nickname Pee Hole Bandit because he liked to brag about his amorous exploits. Pee Hole was friendly, wore tailored camouflage jumpsuits, and smiled a lot. You would never know by meeting him that he was Tan Phu's chief interrogator.

I went over to the LLDB commo bunker to meet my counterpart, Dih Dah. He was a thin, serious soldier, and was furiously beating out a message in Vietnamese Morse code when I walked in. The Vietnamese rhythm and style on the key sounded completely unintelligible to me, but Dih Dah seemed to be communicating on his old AN/GRC-9 radio all right. When he finished his message we had a short conversation using his limited English and our mutually limited French. Before I left, he showed me several batteries for the PRC-10 field radio. "You give me new battery?" he asked. I didn't know it at the time, but this would get to be a very familiar refrain.

After these introductions, we were given a tour of the camp's defenses and briefed on the tactical situation. Neither the situation nor the defenses did much to make us feel very secure. To the north and west of camp ran the canals. Directly across the canal on the west was the village of Tan Phu, and along the banks of both canals, vision and fields of fire were blocked by houses and vegetation. The old road ran down the south side of the canal to our north. A footbridge connected our camp to the village, and a partially destroyed steel-girder bridge crossed the canal to the north.

To the south and east stretched a wide-open rice paddy that afforded good fields of fire and also provided us a handy drop zone. An open area just outside the front gate of camp was the helicopter landing pad.

"We have several problems with constructing defenses," Captain Lewis, the A-20 team leader, was saying as we walked around the perimeter. "Down here in the Delta, you hit water after you dig down about one foot, so everything has to be built aboveground." He pointed out the water-filled ditch in front of the earthen berm that surrounded the camp. "It gave us a moat, but that's the only good point."

The side of the berm facing away from camp was studded with sharpened *punji* stakes, and about twenty meters in front of this was the first of two rows of double-apron barbed wire. The wire had trip flares attached to it, but there were no land mines between the fences. "If we put out mines," Lewis said, "the grass grows up, blocks the field of fire, and we can't get in to cut it."

Tan Phu was laid out as a simple rectangle. A machine-gun bunker with overhead cover was at each corner, and another position was dug into the berm between each of these. Most of the emplacements looked pretty dilapidated. "All building material for fortification is hard to get," Lewis said. "They won't give us steel planking because it is all being used to build runways. Concrete can only be used for civic action construction projects in the village. Even sandbags are in short supply. We have a standing request for more wire and pickets, and as that comes in you'll be able to add a few more double-apron fences."

In the northern corner of the camp, nearest the intersection of the two canals, stood a thirty-foot-tall watchtower along with a cement blockhouse and a small masonry building that had a red tile roof. "Those are left over from the French," Lewis continued. "The district chief had a squad of men occupying the position up to last year, then the Cong overran 'em and killed them all." The steel door to the blockhouse was riddled with bullet holes. Inside, the walls were also pockmarked by the impact of shrapnel and automatic-weapons fire. "The VC pinned them down, then crawled up and tossed grenades through the firing ports," Lewis told us.

Captain Lewis said there was a .30 caliber machine gun up in the tower. "Bet you could really reach out with a .50 cal from up there," Lieutenant Rowe suggested.

"Can't get 'em," Lewis said. "Everyone at higher levels figures it's just a matter of time before we get overrun, and the flyboys don't want heavy machine guns falling into enemy hands." We stopped in the shade next to the blockhouse. "The rules are that we can't have anything larger than 81-millimeter mortars, nothing bigger than a 57 recoilless rifle, and no heavy machine guns. It's sort of stupid, because we have intel that the units around here already have .50 cals and Russian 12-millimeter machine guns, 75 recoilless, and 82-millimeter mortars." Lewis smiled grimly. "We've also identified battalion- and even regimental-size units, so basically you'll be outnumbered and outgunned."

"What kind of tactical air support can we expect to get?" Leites asked.

"What's available is in short supply and hard to get," Lewis said. "We have very low priority for everything. The Vietnamese Air Force has some armed T-28 trainers that carry machine guns and rockets. An American adviser flies in the backseat, so you have someone to talk to. You won't get air support unless there is some real shit going on. One or two T-28s usually fly support for the airdrops when they come in, and they might hit a target for you if you have one. They practically never fly after dark, though, and that's when you'll need them most."

VandeBerg asked what the situation was on getting a medical evacuation. "U.S. assets will bust their ass coming in to get an American," Lewis said. "They'll even fly in at night if it's a real life-or-death situation. Sometimes they'll come in for one of the LLDB too. For your CIDG, though, you might as well forget it. The CIDG have to depend on Vietnamese assets, and they have zero priority. Basically, you'll have to take care of them the best you can . . . that's what we're trained for, right?"

We started walking back toward the other end of camp and stopped at one of the machine-gun bunkers. The CIDG gunner on duty snapped to attention and smartly saluted as we approached. Ponce inspected the gun. "Looks pretty clean," he said. "What are the troops like?" he asked Lewis. "Do they fight or run?"

Lewis chuckled. "Actually they do a little of both. We have all Vietnamese and a few Cambodes. No Yards this far south. We've put the more experienced troops in the leadership positions, and some are real good. One of the company commanders fought at Dien Bien Phu with the French. Many of them have no prior military experience at all. The Cambodians are generally good, aggressive troops, but there is a lot of friction between them and the Vietnamese. You also have to figure that a certain percentage of the strike force are probably VC. Phong and Pee Hole do a pretty good job of weeding them out, but you'll need to be careful." Lewis patted the .45 on his hip. "Best get in the habit of always going armed."

Lewis took us over to one of two 81mm mortar

positions. A waist-high wall of dirt and sandbags was built in a circle around the tube, and a small ammo storage bunker was built into one wall. "We have two 81s," he told us. "The Americans control this one and the LLDB fire the other one. You'll be doing a lot of shooting, especially at night. Don't count too much on the LLDB for fire support, 'cause they can't hit shit."

In the center of the camp were several rows of palm thatch buildings. We ducked inside the one on the northern end, and it was a little cooler out of the direct sun. "This is the mess hall," Lewis said, "we call it the Hepatitis Tavern." Picnic-style tables stood in the center of the room, and an old, kerosene refrigerator was in one corner. The floors were packed dirt, but they had been swept clean. Several charcoal hibachis stood against one wall. A grinning Vietnamese man dressed only in a pair of dirty black shorts came up and bowed. "This is Hai, our cook," Lewis said. "We suspect he's a VC, but he cooks pretty good." Hai just giggled and nodded, ashes from his cigarette flying everywhere. When Lewis mentioned that Hai was from Cholon, Rowe rattled off something to the cook in Chinese. Hai replied and bowed again, looking a bit surprised.

"First chance I've had to use my Chinese since language school," Rowe said. "Guess I haven't forgotten it yet."

The large room next to the Titis Tavern was filled with canvas cots. Each cot was fitted with a mosquito net. "This is the main sleeping area," Lewis said, "but we've spread our men around a little so one round won't get us all like it did at the B-team. A couple of men sleep in the operations room, the medics sleep in the dispensary, and one radio operator sleeps next to the commo bunker."

I noticed a slight movement over in a dark corner and looked just in time to spot the biggest damned snake I'd ever seen come slithering out. It was as big around as my leg and at least seven feet long. "That's Harvey, our pet rock python," Lewis told us. "We'll leave him with you. He catches a lot of rats." Harvey ignored us and crawled under one of the cots.

Our tour continued and we next visited the combination supply room/armory. "We control all the supplies, of course," Lewis was saying, but I suddenly wasn't paying much attention. I was looking at the rows and rows of weapons that filled one wall. Being a real gun nut, I felt like a kid in a candy store.

When the CIDG program originally started, many of the strike forces were armed with the 9mm family of submachine guns. The slightly built Vietnamese had liked these because of the weapon's small size and light weight. The 9mm didn't have much range or punch, though, and since most of the other Vietnamese military units were armed with WWII-era American small arms, there had also been a problem with ammunition interchangeability and resupply.

By the time Tan Phu opened, the 9mm weapons were no longer issued. Our troops were armed with a wide variety of weapons ranging from the '03 Springfield and model '97 riot gun, to the M-2A1 carbine. I drooled as I looked at the mint-condition Garands, Thompsons, and M-3 "grease guns" in our armory. Several of the '03 Springfields were the rare, sniper version with Weaver scope and an added cheek rest. Some of the weapons were still in Cosmoline and had probably been in storage since the 1940s.

Although the U.S. Army had by this time converted to

the M-60 machine gun, out at the CIDG camps we still had the .30 caliber Browning M-1919 and the BAR. These were big, heavy weapons, and our average CIDG striker weighed about 100 pounds. Even the M-1 Garand was too big a weapon for a Vietnamese troop, but we didn't have a lot of control over what type of weapons the supply types in the rear sent out to us.

The light-weapons NCO from A-20 told us that none of the '03 Springfields had yet been issued to the strike force, although he'd had plans to train a few snipers and use the old bolt-action rifles strictly in a defensive role. Although the M-3 and the Thompson were smaller and easier to carry than the Garand, they were even heavier, and with a basic load of .45 ammo, they really weighted the little troops down. Most of the strikers took the butt stocks off the Thompson to make it lighter, thus reducing its accuracy a good deal. The carbine was just the right size and weight for our troops; unfortunately, there weren't enough of them to go around.

As it was, the type of weapon a striker carried was sort of a status symbol. There were a few of the M-2A1 carbines around camp, but these were equally divided between the American and Vietnamese Special Forces teams. The M-2A1 not only had a selector switch allowing full automatic fire, but also a folding stock. Next in desirability was the plain M-2 carbine. The M-2 didn't have a folding stock, but did have a selector switch. The M-2s went only to company commanders and platoon leaders. A few of the remaining troops were lucky enough to get the semiautomatic M-1 model of the carbine. The other strikers had to carry Thompsons, M-3s, or the Garand. Down at the bottom of the pecking order were the poor bastards who had to lug around the BARs and the machine guns.

The CIDG company commanders and platoon leaders were issued .45 pistols. Both the U.S. and Vietnamese Special Forces team members also carried side arms, and in this area, some of the LLDB were one up on the Americans. While the U.S. team had to settle for the standard Colt M-1911, many of the LLDB carried the highly desirable Browning high-powered 9mm. Since there was no longer any 9mm ammo in the supply system, it was occasionally possible to con one of the LLDB into trading pistols.

"Right now the basic issue for a new striker is two sets of tiger-stripe fatigues, a flop hat, a belt, one pair of Batta boots, one canteen, one of these indigenous rucksacks, some web gear, and a weapon. We have a ton of underwear and socks, but we stopped issuing them because no one will wear them," Captain Lewis said, continuing the tour. "Someone on your detachment will have to be assigned as a supply sergeant. Most of the teams are using the junior demo man for that job." I wondered what Martin would think about that when and if he came back.

"Your team members will want to find a few sets of cammies to wear on operations," Lewis went on. "The tiger-stripe fatigues don't come in sizes large enough for the bigger guys, but we have a few sets in the old leopard pattern that will fit." VandeBerg, our ex-Marine, was smiling approvingly, because these were the same style camouflage fatigues the Marines had worn in WWII. Once a jarhead, always a jarhead, I thought to myself.

We moved into the room that served as the operations center and crowded around the large situation map on the wall. Lewis threw back the curtain that concealed it and pointed to an area on the map just west of camp. There were many symbols drawn in red, which indicated enemy units. "This is the U Minh forest. No government forces have gone in there for years, and the VC completely control it. Basically the situation around here is that we mostly run things during daylight, but the VC are in charge at night. We're trying to extend our control to include night too, but it's going to take a while."

Lewis pointed to a blue rectangle several kilometers to our south at another major canal intersection. "This is the district headquarters, Thoi Binh. They have two 155 howitzers down there, and they've been pretty good at giving us fire support. It's a strictly Vietnamese outfit, though, so everything has to be requested and coordinated through the LLDB."

Rowe asked if they could hit anything. "They aren't bad," Lewis said. He indicated the crossed cannons on Rowe's collar. "They could probably use a little help from an American artillery officer, though."

"What kind of security do they have on those guns, sir?" Ponce asked, echoing what all of us were thinking. If the 155s fell into enemy hands, they could wipe out our camp in a matter of minutes.

"Not much, I'm afraid," Lewis said grimly. "They only have about a platoon. They don't get attacked often, though. Maybe the Cong are afraid of the guns."

It was late afternoon by then and time to start preparing the daily situation report, or sitrep. We broke off the briefing to clean up and get ready for a special dinner of water buffalo steak that Hai had prepared for us. As the sun set dramatically behind the U Minh, we got ready to spend our first night at Tan Phu.

Chapter 6

That evening, the LLDB were hosting a party for the Americans down at the CIDG canteen. We had a meeting before we walked down to that end of the camp and were assigned positions to go to in the event of an alert or attack. The "nightly haps," as we called them, were a normal part of life around Tan Phu. My position was the commo bunker, Ponce and Lowe would go to the 81 position, and the medics would head for the masonry building, which was the camp dispensary. Carey's position was near the ammo bunker, Hardy was assigned a strategic machine-gun bunker on the east wall, and the officers were to float around where needed.

The U.S. team always kept one person on guard all night also. The outgoing A-20 said they'd pull it that night, and that we could pick up the duty the next night. "It's not too bad with a full detachment," Lewis told us. "We've been starting our guard roster at 1100 hours and ending it at 0600. Each man pulls one hour, so every few days you get some nights off."

There were two outdoor shower stalls at Tan Phu. Fifty-five-gallon drums had been rigged with shower-heads and hoisted up on platforms. At three every afternoon our team laundry man, Big Boy, went out and lit a charcoal fire under each drum, so there was plenty of warm water. We took turns using the facilities, then brought chairs out in the open area outside the team building to enjoy the brief period of peace and quiet in the evening twilight before it was time for the party.

The LLDB detachment met us down at the CIDG canteen and introduced us to the strike force company commanders and platoon leaders. We were also introduced to the two Vietnamese beers, 33 and La Rue, which were served over ice. Phong made a speech, then Lewis and Leites were each required to say a few words. After a second round of the beer, which was pretty potent stuff, items of food were brought forth. There were things like dried squid, frog egg soup, and other dishes that I couldn't identify. I wished I'd had another round of beer before trying to gag it all down.

The party was just starting to get mellow when, from across the canal to the west, there was a sudden burst of machine-gun fire and the *crump-crump* of exploding 60mm mortar rounds. I was still a little jumpy from the attack at the B-team and almost crawled under the table before I noticed that none of the old-timers appeared too concerned. In a moment or two a striker came hurrying in and rattled off a quick briefing to Phong and Canh. The strike force company commanders and platoon leaders muttered apologies and hurried out.

"I think must end party now," Phong told us. "Our western outpost is under attack, and they might need our help."

As I hurried through the still-unfamiliar darkness toward the commo bunker, the intensity of fire across the canal grew. Five or six stray rounds from a machine gun cracked far overhead, but I instinctively ducked. I heard a *thunk* from our 81 and an illumination round popped over the battle area. There was a brief lull for a second or two after the flare lit up the night, and I could hear the whistling sound the canister made as it dropped to the ground. Then the battle continued at increased volume.

"Welcome to Tan Phu," the A-20 radio operator said to me over his shoulder as I ducked into the bunker. He had been sending in the evening sitrep when the firing started and had already alerted the B-team that we were under attack. "This is pretty normal around here," he told me. "I'll let you take over the commo tomorrow, and when you get a chance to study the signal instructions, you'll see that we have brevity codes to cover just about every possibility. What I just sent in was this one here." He pointed to a list of words taped to the wall. "You send in 'Big Daddy' and the B-team knows it means you're under an attack of unknown intensity and that they should stand by for further developments."

At the top of the list of code words, written in large red letters, was the phrase Flaming Arrow. "That's the one you send if your shit is really in the wind," he told me. "It means you need an air strike ASAP and that he should look for the fire arrow." Each A-detachment in Vietnam had a large arrow out in an open area that could be seen from the air. The arrow was on a swivel so it could be pointed in different directions and was outlined with tin cans filled with sand and gasoline. Once burning, the arrow was easily spotted from above, and the pilot knew that it pointed toward the enemy. The number of burning pots in the tail section of the arrow indicated how many meters away from the camp the enemy was.

The firing had tapered off, and from outside I heard the commotion as several wounded CIDG were carried into camp. VandeBerg would be busy that night, I thought.

The field phone in the bunker rang and it was Captain Leites. "Looks like we're back to 'all clear.' Tell the B-team we have three CIDG wounded in action. Enemy casualties unknown. We'll have more details in tomorrow's situation report."

It was midnight when we decided to turn in. We were warned to make sure the mosquito nets were securely tucked in around the bottom of the bed. "It's not the mosquitoes you need to worry about as much as the rats," one of the A-20 medics told us. "They sometimes try to gnaw on you when you're asleep, and if you get a rat bite, it means an automatic series of rabies shots!"

Even though I was exhausted, the adrenaline was still flowing through my body and I had a hard time drifting off to sleep. My sense of hearing seemed to have become suddenly very acute, and every little thump or bump from around the camp sounded just like an enemy mortar being fired. Finally, around 0100 hours, I managed to drift off, only to be jerked out of sleep almost immediately.

"What the hell?" Hardy suddenly yelled. "Oh, shit!" There were crashing sounds as Hardy tried to roll out of his cot, became entangled in the mosquito net, and pulled the whole works over with him.

A brief period of pandemonium followed as everyone around us woke and started grabbing for their guns and equipment. Someone turned on a flashlight, and although the lens was covered with a red filter, there was enough light to see Hardy by his overturned cot and to spot just the tail of Harvey as he slithered off into the shadows.

"The damned snake tried to crawl in bed with me!" Hardy said.

There were a few titters from the A-20 team members. "Sorry, we forgot to warn you about that," someone on their team said in the darkness. "Sometimes Harvey gets cold at night and likes to snuggle up to some body heat."

I really zonked out after that, and it seemed like I'd only been asleep for a second or two when someone was shaking me awake. There was the sound of jangling equipment and running feet. "Get up!" the person shaking me said. "We got some more haps." I groggily grabbed my carbine and web gear, which was on the floor next to my cot, and stumbled back to the commo bunker.

This time the A-20 radio operator let me send in the alert message. It was a little after 0400 hours, and at that time in the morning the airways were fairly clear. I heard our 81 fire a round of illumination, then, after a pause, it spit out three quick rounds of HE. The target wasn't very far away, because I could plainly hear the sharp concussions as the rounds detonated.

Lieutenant Rowe came in the bunker and told us that one of our night ambush patrols had made contact. A squad of enemy had stumbled into the killing zone of the ambush, and so far our men were reporting one confirmed VC KIA and no friendly casualties. We sent the signal for "all clear" to the B-detachment at about 0500, and I didn't even bother trying to get back to sleep after that.

At dawn the night ambush patrol returned to camp, triumphantly carrying the dead VC as a grisly trophy. They dumped the body in the middle of the village market and brought the captured weapon to us in our tactical operations center. It was an American carbine, probably one originally captured from us.

Hai came to work from his home in the village and started cooking breakfast. My first night at Tan Phu was over, and I had only about 179 more to go.

Chapter 7

The next morning we toured the network of outposts that surrounded the camp. "The way we've got it set up right now," Captain Lewis explained, "one company stays in the camp and the other company pulls outpost duty." One platoon of thirty men was stationed in Tan Phu village itself, while squads were scattered around outside the camp in defensive positions, guarding the likely avenues of enemy approach. This was lonely, dangerous duty, and I didn't envy those strikers who spent the nights out there.

Every night, the camp also sent out several ambush patrols consisting of five or six men each. The patrols left camp at dusk, moved into their ambush positions just before dark, then returned to camp in the morning. Each patrol carried radios, trip flares, and a claymore mine. We suspected that some of these patrols simply found a good place to hide and slept all night, but occasionally they killed some VC.

After lunch I joined the A-20 radio operators and worked with them the rest of the day. They showed me the camp commo setup and answered my questions concerning the Signal Operating Instructions, or SOI. The commo bunker at Tan Phu was one of the better-built bunkers in camp, but like all the fortifications there, it was built completely aboveground. Two wooden retaining walls a couple of feet apart had been filled with sandbags and loose dirt. A sandbag roof several feet thick was supported by wooden beams. The entire bunker had been constructed inside the large thatch building that also held the operations center and the supply room. This not only kept it dry, but concealed it from view.

In 1963 the standard-issue radio for Special Forces A-teams was the AN/GRC-109, and it was our lifeline with higher headquarters and any outside support. This radio had originally been designed during the latter part of WWII especially for guerrilla warfare applications. The radio was in four components the size of shoe boxes, and consisted of a transmitter, a receiver, and two power supplies. The radio could operate on a variety of AC or DC current, including a hand-cranked generator. The 109 transmitted only Morse code, but could receive code or voice. It put out fifteen watts of power, but with the right antennas and using skip-wave, radio-wave propagation, it had a transmission range of about two thousand miles . . . in theory, that is.

The AN/GRC-109 was excellent in its intended role as a clandestine, guerrilla radio. For the mission Special Forces found itself performing in Vietnam, however, it was inadequate. Each A-team in Vietnam was located from fifty to one hundred miles from its supporting B-detachment. This was too close for skip-wave propagation and too far for the fifteen-watt ground wave.

The airwaves in Southeast Asia were very cluttered with interference, some of it intentional enemy jamming. In radio terms, a signal is rated from one to five for strength and readability, with five being the clearest. At Tan Phu we seldom went above a readability of 3×3, which would translate as "fair."

Most radio traffic to and from higher headquarters was first encrypted using what was known as a "one-time pad." The receiving and sending stations each had a duplicate booklet with random five-letter groups of letters. The messages were first written under these random groups, then transposed using a standard "tri-graph." Each page in the crypto pad was different, and each was used only one time, so the system was secure enough for our needs. It was very time-consuming to encrypt and decrypt messages, however, and to me this job was never more than boring drudgery.

The A-teams were required to make only one or two scheduled radio contacts a day. In the mornings, we sent in a weather report of conditions in our areas and any other important information. We received any traffic the B-team might have for us, such as the ETA of aircraft for the day. The A-team radio operators were then free to help do the many jobs required around the camp until late afternoon, when it was time to start encrypting the daily sitrep.

The sitrep was the most important message of the day, and was prepared by the combined efforts of the two officers and the two operations and intelligence NCOs. It covered everything of importance that had occurred during the previous twenty-four hours and was divided into two sections, one on operations and one on intelligence. At Tan Phu my scheduled time to send the daily sitrep was between 1730 and 1800 hours. I tried to get the message from the O&I section no later than 1600 hours, because sometimes the sitreps would be quite lengthy and I needed time to encode them.

The radio airwaves were always the most cluttered and the signal strength always weakest during evening hours when we had to send in these messages, and the daily sitrep soon became a chore I dreaded.

For tactical communications with patrols, outposts, and combat operations around camp, we had the PRC-10 radio and the HT-1. The PRC-10 was a Korean War–vintage radio that was difficult to tune. If it was working right, the 10 had a range of one or two kilometers using the standard whip antenna. We had big problems with the dry cell batteries we received for this radio. Most of them had been pulled from old war stock and had been lying around hot warehouses for many years. One out of every three of these batteries was completely dead right out of the wrapper, and none of them still had a full charge. We had no way of testing these batteries other than putting them in a radio and seeing if they worked. Sometimes they might hold a charge for only two or three transmissions, and sometimes they might last several days.

The HT-1 was a radio that had been developed especially for paramilitary units in Vietnam. It was a simple, inexpensive little radio with one preset frequency and a built-in telescoping antenna. The HT-1, made of black plastic, was about the size of a carton of cigarettes and ran on eight flashlight batteries. It had a one-mile range and was fairly dependable.

There was other communications equipment in the standard Army supply system that might have helped us a lot at the A-team level, but like so many other things, we couldn't get it. The standard-issue ground plane antenna, known as a "two-niner-two," would have been a big help in extending the range of the PRC-10s and HT-1s, but since these weren't TO&E-issue items for

A-teams, they were unavailable. We knew how to make improvised "jungle antennas," of course, and did so, but these never worked as well as the real thing. The only 292 in camp belonged to the LLDB.

The electric power for Tan Phu came from a five-KW gas generator, and I found myself in charge of it and the rest of the camp electrical system. The jobs around camp were broken down in large, general categories, many of them far from what we had been trained for or knew much about. If it involved electricity, for example, it was commo's job.

Encoding and sending in my first sitrep was difficult and nerve-racking. Because of the two attacks the night before and the change of detachments at camp, there was a lot of information to report, and the message was quite long and involved. It took me two hours to encrypt the message, and I went well over my allotted thirty-minute time frame in sending it. I was the new guy on the radio net, and I could feel the impatience of Net Control at the B-team and of the other waiting A-detachments as I tapped out the message. I was using the standard radio procedure that I'd learned in commo school and was not yet used to all the shortcuts and idiosyncrasies of the net I was on. Besides that, my code speed was only about eighteen words per minute, and the more experienced guys on the net wanted to work faster. The B-team operator and several of the other A-teams on the net were using automatic keyers, or "bugs," and I wasn't used to copying the code these keyers produced either.

I finally got my sitrep sent and acknowledged, then copied a message telling us what time the choppers would arrive the next day to take the A-20 team members back to Can Tho. We were also alerted to a scheduled air-drop of supplies due to arrive the following week. The message ended with the good news that, except for Sergeant Kemmer, the rest of our wounded detachment members were being treated in Nha Trang and would be sent back to us in a week or two.

I was especially glad to hear this, because I was anxious for Cross to get back to help me with the communications duties. Sidney was a better radio operator than I was, and more important, he really liked the job. I preferred doing almost anything else on the team other than my primary job and was looking forward to going out on my first combat operation. Because I was the only radio operator, I couldn't leave camp until Cross returned.

The guys from A-20 were in high spirits after I relayed the message to them confirming their departure via helicopter the next morning. They had completely turned things over to us by then and were basically spending their last night in camp as our guests. I knew it must feel good to be out from under most of the responsibility.

That night was quiet at Tan Phu, one of the few such nights we ever spent. I pulled guard duty from 0200 to 0300 and passed my time killing some of the huge, voracious rats that always appeared as soon as it got dark. In our mess hall someone had made a stab at decoration by hanging the orange and white canopy of a cargo parachute as a false ceiling. Occasionally rats would crawl around on top of the chute, their body weight making telltale bulges I could see from below. I found a big stick and discovered what a wonderful feeling it was to tee off on the slimy creatures as they walked unsuspectingly overhead.

About 1000 the next morning two helicopters arrived to take A-20 back to Can Tho. They also brought our mail, which had already started catching up with us, and took our outgoing letters. We shook hands with the old team, then they boarded the choppers and took off. The HU-1Bs circled the camp one time, then disappeared toward the B-team. For better or for worse, A-23 was fully on its own.

The next few days went quickly as we fell into the routine of life at Tan Phu. As soon as the old team was gone, we were deluged with requests from the LLDB and the CIDG for all manner of supplies and equipment. The troops figured that since we were new, we could more easily be suckered into coughing up the items they suspected we were hoarding in the supply room. The fact of the matter was that we really didn't have most of the things they wanted, and being old soldiers ourselves, we weren't as naive in these matters as they thought anyway.

We had a visit from the B-team commander, and he brought word that our men in the hospital at Nha Trang were all doing well, with the exception of PFC Martin, who had already been evicted. It seems that Martin had gotten into an altercation with one of the hospital medics and had threatened to kill him. The threat was taken seriously, because Bill had chased the poor medic clear out of the hospital and down to the beach. The hospital staff decided that if Martin was well enough to do that, he was well enough to be discharged. The last anyone knew of him, Bill caught a ride on a helicopter with the C-team commander and was somewhere in-country trying to make his way to Tan Phu.

The first of the month rolled around, and that brought payday for our troops. We had been thoroughly briefed on what to expect, but our first actual experience of paying the CIDG was more difficult than any of us figured. On the last day of July a chopper arrived and delivered a big, metal ammo can filled with piasters. As the XO, Lieutenant Rowe was also the pay officer, and after the money was carefully counted, he signed for it. Of course, all our troops knew what had arrived, and camp morale suddenly rose to fever pitch.

The CIDG were basically mercenary troops, not really part of the regular Vietnamese Army, and all their equipment and pay came directly through American channels. They actually made more working for us than they would have as ARVN soldiers, and it took care of their military obligation too. On the other hand, the LLDB were officially in command of the CIDG camps, with the American Special Forces supposedly there only as advisers.

This situation caused a lot of friction, especially around payday, because the LLDB and the entire strike force chain of command assumed and expected to get their normal kickbacks and graft from the system each time the troops were paid. This was simply the normal course of events to the Vietnamese, as common to them as it is to an American who tips a waiter. Each payday became a tense, stressful circus, with the American team trying to make sure everything was on the up-and-up and the Vietnamese all trying to gouge out what they considered their rightful cut of the loot.

We ran pay at Tan Phu just like we used to in the old American Army. An American team member, usually Rowe, sat at a table and personally gave each CIDG member his money. The individual was checked off the camp roster and had to sign for his pay. The most popular scam the Vietnamese tried to run was to claim that certain individuals could not personally be present to sign for their money because they were on outpost duty, or sick, or on leave, or some other lame excuse. Of course, the soldier's squad leader or some other representative was always there to gladly sign for and pick up the missing man's pay. Yeah, right!

What this usually meant was that the missing man was a "ghost" on the roster and had either never existed or had once been a member but was now gone, or that he perhaps owed some sort of kickback or gratuity to the man attempting to sign for the pay. The trouble was, even though we knew what was going on, occasionally the missing man really *was* out on some official duty, and the soldier asking to sign for his pay was actually a good, honest person. Paying the troops at an A-team required a lot of sound, on-the-spot decisions and finesse. Trying to keep things too scrupulously honest could start serious trouble, as the American team at Tan Phu was soon to discover.

A few days after payday I got a message that the expected airdrop was on the way. The message told what supplies were being parachuted in, what type of aircraft to expect, and what time they would arrive. I was also sent the air-to-ground radio frequency the pilot would be using.

The job of managing an incoming air resupply at Tan Phu was usually allotted to the communications and demolitions sections. Communications was necessary with the aircraft, and the two demo/engineer sergeants had picked up the extra duty of controlling the camp's supplies. An air resupply was always a fairly complicated operation and involved a squad or so to secure the drop zone, labor parties to bring in the supplies as they were dropped, someone to talk to the pilots, and other people to watch the labor detail to ensure they didn't steal anything before it reached camp.

The Tan Phu DZ was a large, open rice paddy on the east side of camp. Our rifle range was out there too, and we often used the area to test-fire different weapons. To the local farmers, however, it was still just a rice paddy, and they doggedly attempted to work the fields when we weren't using them for military purposes. I suppose that because they'd been farming it for the last three thousand years, they figured they still had the right to do so.

As it drew near the time for our first airdrop, I noticed that ten or twenty farmers were out working their field. I had one of the interpreters with me and told him to order them away from the area. The interpreter climbed up to the top of the camp berm and began yelling and waving his arms, but the farmers appeared deaf and completely ignored him. About this time the grinning, LLDB intel sergeant, Pee Hole, happened to come strolling by.

He stood with me for a while with an amused look on his face as he watched the yelling and gesticulating interpreter, then took the Thompson from a nearby striker and climbed up on the berm. "You want farmer move, you do this way," he told me, then fired off half the Thompson's magazine directly over the heads of the hardworking men and women in the field. The drop zone was empty in about thirty seconds.

"Farmer number-hucking-ten," Pee Hole told me as he handed the striker back his weapon. Being a soldier myself, I tended to agree with him, but I could also see that this probably wasn't the best way to win a lot of hearts and minds.

The C-123 flew in right on time and was accompanied

by a T-28. They buzzed the camp first, and Carey, who was in charge of the DZ party, threw a green smoke grenade into the middle of the field. "We've popped smoke," I said into the PRC-10 handset from my perch on one of the camp's machine-gun bunkers.

"Roger," came the pilot's reply, "I identify green."

"Affirmative," I told him, "drop the stuff right on the smoke, over."

The C-123 began making passes and kicking bundles out the tailgate, while the T-28 zoomed around aggressively. The load was mostly barbed wire and steel fence pickets for our defenses. On the last pass the DZ was covered with men from the labor detail who were busily breaking down the pallets and porting in the supplies. As the extraction chute jerked out the last load, it broke apart just as it cleared the tailgate, and the air was suddenly filled with hundreds of six-foot-long steel spears hurtling toward the ground.

The men on the ground saw this and began running every which way, yelling with terror and waving their arms while at the same time trying to look overhead to dodge the deadly falling objects. All the strikers who happened to be watching from safe areas started laughing hysterically, and I have to admit that I did too. It was really very funny if you didn't happen to be out in the middle of the drop zone. Luckily no one got hit, although there were some near misses, and after it was over, the men who had nearly been killed thought it was funny too.

After the last pass, the planes buzzed the camp once more, this time at about forty feet. The T-28 flew over inverted, the Vietnamese in the front seat waving gaily and the American in the backseat pretending to read a magazine.

Chapter 8

By the second week in August our wounded had returned from the hospital, and except for still needing a new team sergeant, A-23 was back up to strength. Heavy recruiting of new CIDG strike force members had added another fifty men. Building and construction of new camp defenses now took a backseat to increased training efforts and to larger, more aggressive combat operations.

Major Phong came over one morning to tell us the new propaganda line that the VC were circulating in the area. "They say that old American team wasn't killing enough villagers and that is why you replaced them," he told us. He also said that bounties had been placed on our heads and we should be very careful.

While convalescing in Nha Trang, Cross had purchased a "bug" from a radio operator who was returning to the States, and we were starting to get up to speed with everyone else on the net. Sidney showed me the wound on his thigh, which was several inches long and held together with heavy wire sutures. For the time being he was physically unable to do much except operate the radio, and this suited me just fine because I was anxious to get away from those duties for a while.

A new operation that would involve three platoons of

CIDG and several American and Vietnamese Special Forces members was in the planning stages, and I volunteered to go along. That afternoon we had a briefing in the operations center and worked out the details.

The tactics we used at Tan Phu were dictated by the terrain and the relative strengths and weaknesses of our CIDG and of the VC units we faced. At this stage in the conflict we did not feel we were ready to run operations of more than one day's duration. The VC really did control things around Tan Phu at night, and attempting to establish overnight defensive positions with our mostly untrained strikers would have been suicidal.

We ran sweeps and hammer-and-anvil operations primarily, depending on surprise and speed to hit the enemy, kill or capture as many as possible, and then move quickly back to camp before they could react with the larger units we knew they were capable of rounding up. Eventually we hoped to increase our strength to the point that we could go to the field for longer periods and slug it out with them, but in that summer of '63, we were a long way from that.

Dan Pitzer and Norm Hardy would be the other Americans going on this operation, and the LLDB were sending Pee Hole and one of their medics. "The operation will depart camp at 0200 hours with two platoons from first company," Captain Leites said, referring us to the large situation map. "All three Americans will accompany First Platoon. Second Platoon will be point element, and the two LLDB will be with them. You'll move northeast along the main canal bank to the intersection with Canal Nine, then turn west and follow it to this location," he said as he indicated a spot on the map and read off the coordinates.

"Third Platoon of Second Company is pulling duty in

the village right now, and they will be your blocking force. They will move out an hour after you and take up positions along Canal Seven."

Pee Hole moved to the map and pointed to a scattering of structures indicated along the banks of Canal Eight, which would lie between our two elements. "We think beaucoup VC stay here," Pee Hole said.

"The trick will be for you to get in position undetected," Leites continued. "Be ready to assault at first light. Try to keep any enemy from running back west toward the U Minh, and push them toward the blocking force."

Sergeant Lowe pointed to the open area between Canal Eight, where we suspected the enemy were, and the position of the blocking force along Canal Seven. "We've registered our 81 mortar on this area and we'll be standing by for fire support," he told us. "If you can push them out in this open rice field, give us a call and we'll have rounds on the way real quick."

"What about support from the 155s at Thoi Binh, sir?" I asked, wondering about the commo problem this would incur.

Leites turned to Rowe. "What do you think?"

Lieutenant Rowe thought it over for a moment, then slowly shook his head. "I don't think so," he said. "I've been working with them, and they're getting better, but I don't like the idea of them trying to shoot that close to our own guys yet."

"About how many Cong do we suspect are there?" Dan asked, probably wondering what Pee Hole's estimate of "beaucoup VC" meant.

"Could be anything from a few strays to a full platoon," Hardy told us.

"What's the commo situation?" Leites asked me.

"Each platoon will have a PRC-10 and will carry several spare batteries," I said. "I'm also taking a 10 just for American use. Sidney will be on standby at this end from the time we leave the gate, and Dih Dah will be monitoring the LLDB net. There shouldn't be any problem maintaining contact at the range we'll be operating from. Cross will be hooked up to the jungle antenna, and the LLDB have their two-niner-two."

"Any backup for the 10s?" Ponce asked with a slight smile. As an ex–radio operator, he knew all about the undependability of the PRC-10.

"Just the HT-1s," I answered.

"That will have to do," Leites said, then asked if there were any questions. Someone asked about uniforms and equipment.

"What individual weapon you want to carry is up to you," Rowe answered. "It's highly advised that Americans try to blend in with the rest of the troops as much as possible, so if you haven't got a set of tiger-stripe cammies yet, try to find some."

After the briefing I went about collecting the items of munitions and equipment I thought I might need for the operation. My first consideration was what weapon to take. I had decided that on this operation I would carry the PRC-10 myself just to make sure I had control of it, so to cut down on any more weight, I picked up one of the folding-stock carbines from the armory. We had only a few thirty-round magazines for the M-2s, and I rounded up as many of these as I could find, loading them with only twenty-eight rounds each. Underloading the magazines reduced the pressure on the magazine spring and helped eliminate feeding problems. I filled the rest of the

space in my ammo pouches with the twenty-round magazines. As an afterthought, I loaded one of these with all
tracers, thinking it might come in handy for signaling.

I attached one smoke and two frag grenades to the harness, then added two canteens, compass, first-aid pouch,
a trench knife, and my pistol. It made quite a load, especially when I added the weight of the radio and its spare
battery. At five feet seven inches tall, I hadn't had any
trouble finding a camouflage uniform to wear, and I
knew that with one of the flop hats covering my brown
hair I would be indistinguishable from one of our strikers
at a distance.

Because I was going on the operation, I didn't have to
pull guard that night, but there was a minor probe of the
outpost line at about midnight that interrupted my sleep.
When VandeBerg shook me awake at 0130, I felt like I
hadn't slept at all. Those of us involved with the operation gathered in the Titis Tavern to grab a quick cup of
coffee and to smear camouflage stick on our faces and
hands.

As we waited for Pee Hole and the LLDB medic to
join us, I passed out the primary, alternate, and air-
to-ground frequencies. Cross and I had invented some
voice call signs to use and also worked out a simple
method to encode short messages. He and I checked and
netted the PRC-10s we'd be using. I'd put a brand-new
battery in my radio just the previous afternoon, but I now
discovered it was dead. I quickly changed batteries and
picked up another spare while steadily cursing under my
breath.

I saw that Hardy and Pitzer had also opted for the carbine, and Dan was carrying his medical aid bag. When
Pee Hole arrived, I noticed he was carrying only a pistol,

but that a striker armed with one of the Model '97 riot guns shadowed him wherever he went.

Outside, the night was pitch-black. The two platoons from First Company were already moving silently out of camp and across the bridge to the west bank of the canal. I mentally noted that their noise discipline wasn't bad and the only sounds were the creaking of web gear and the occasional clunk as a piece of equipment accidentally struck something. They stopped in the village and waited for us.

Pee Hole and his medic moved forward to the lead platoon while Dan, Norm, and I positioned ourselves with the trail element as planned. We waited for several minutes for the unit to move out, but nothing happened. Finally Pee Hole walked back to us. "We go now?" he asked Hardy. Our real position now became apparent. We weren't advisers at all, but leaders.

Norm nodded in the affirmative. *"Di-di,"* he said, and the column started winding its way through the dark, tropical night.

Most trees and other vegetation in the Delta grew along the banks of the canals, and there was plenty of it. Palms, bamboo, elephant grass, and mango were in abundance. All the buildings were also on the banks, the inhabitants using the canals not only for their transportation system, but also for washing and for a handy sewer. Once out of the immediate area of Tan Phu, the loyalty of the inhabitants of the small clusters of huts we passed became more and more suspect.

These people were peasants and farmers and came from a long line of such people. Most of them were actually neutral in the war we and the communists waged, wanting only to be left alone to go about their quiet, rural lives. For generations these farmers had simply gone with the flow of history, pretending to support whoever was strongest, but actually not caring about any of it. Most of the cottages we passed kept two sets of flags. When the Diem forces were in the area, they broke out the government flags, and when we were out of the area and the VC came back, they quickly replaced the progovernment paraphernalia with Viet Cong trappings. There were so many coming and going of forces, however, that sometimes they forgot who was who and got caught with the wrong stuff on their walls.

Now as we walked along the slippery mud of the trail, the houses we passed were dark. Our progress had been marked by the barking of dogs and the squawk of geese many of the villagers kept as watch animals, however, and I knew our passing did not go unnoticed. We had eight canal crossings to make before we reached Number Nine, and the column came to a halt as we approached the first of these.

Many of our untrained troops simply stood where they were, holding whispered conversations. The other Americans and I, along with several of the more experienced CIDG, moved up and down the column showing them how to take cover at the edge of the trail with their weapons covering our flanks.

For the first time I noticed a short, stocky striker who had been sticking close to me since the march began. He was wearing a .45, so I knew he must be the platoon leader. I was beginning to wonder why it was taking us so long to get moving again, when, as if reading my mind, the platoon leader whispered to me, "VC take away bridge at night."

While the bridge was being repaired, I took the time to

make a short commo check with camp, and Cross came in loud and clear. The column began to move slowly forward again, and when I got to the crossing point, I found that the bridge I had to negotiate was a single piece of wet, muddy, slippery bamboo. We crossed one man at a time, and even though the strikers had been doing this sort of thing all their lives, about every fourth one slipped and fell in the dirty water. I was wearing the new American jungle boots, and their treads were full of mud. This made my crossing even more treacherous, but somehow I accomplished it without falling in. The platoon leader was waiting for me on the other side of the bank and had watched me cross. "Number one," he said, grinning, revealing a mouthful of gold teeth.

The farther we got from camp, the farther we were moving into what was enemy territory. There was something primal about moving through the black, tropical night with the real danger of death lurking in every shadow, and I could actually feel all my physical senses grow and expand. Because my eyesight was limited by the dark, I became aware of my heightened sense of hearing and of smell, and I caught myself occasionally sniffing the rich, scent-laden air like an animal. Somehow, it was not an unpleasant feeling.

In spite of having to slow down at each canal crossing, we made good time. At Canal Eight, starting to feel overconfident at my ability to negotiate the bamboo pole bridges, I slipped at the far end and went in. Luckily, I was near the bank and only submerged up to my waist, which kept the radio out of the water. My carbine was in my right hand, however, and it briefly went under. There were snickers from nearby strikers as I waded up the bank, feeling the silty canal water squishing in my boots.

At the intersection of Canal Nine we took a longer break to rest and regroup. I made another commo check with camp and discovered that I could get through only by putting up the long whip antenna. I didn't like this, because it meant I would be out of radio contact during the actual assault itself. The enemy knew that a radio marked a command element, and the long antenna would draw too much fire.

From this point we turned back to the west, which took us even deeper into enemy country, and movement was much slower. The VC used many booby traps and *punjis*, both as early warning and to harass and slow down any government troops brave enough to venture into their area. The VC's ingenuity at making these booby traps never ceased to amaze me.

They manufactured *dap loi*, a version of a "toe-popper" mine, out of discarded .50 caliber and 20mm shell casings. The shells were reloaded with a homemade primer, black powder, and small chunks of shrapnel, then the mouths of the cases were sealed with wax. The little mines were then placed in bamboo tubes that had a nail tip in the bottom and were buried with just the mouth of the cartridge aboveground. When stepped on, the primer was pushed against the nail, setting it off and sending the charge ripping through the unlucky soldier's foot. The part that really surprised me was the homemade primer. I never have figured out how they manufactured primers in those jungle workshops.

The first hints of dawn were appearing in the east as we stopped once more. Pee Hole walked back to us again, and we had a brief, whispered conference. Our target, the cluster of huts along Canal Eight, now lay about two hundred meters to our south. At the moment, we were shielded from view by the mass of growth along the bank of Canal Nine where we had stopped. As soon as we moved thirty or forty meters toward our objective, however, we would be out of our concealment and into wide-open rice paddy. We decided to move closer to the target while it was still dark, regroup along one of the many dikes, then assault at first light.

Our two platoons formed a long skirmish line, and we began slowly and carefully making our way through the thick foliage at the edge of the trail. If we set off any booby traps at this point, the game would be up and our quarry would be alerted. Nothing exploded, and I emerged from a stand of reeds to suddenly find myself in the clear. To the right and left of me I saw the rest of the unit break into the open, then I stepped off the low dike I was on and into the shallow water of the rice paddy. Carbine now at the ready, I began moving toward the ominous, dark line of trees that marked the suspected location of the enemy.

The water was not deep, only up to about midcalf, but walking was still not easy. There were occasional holes and low spots where I would suddenly sink up to my waist. My uniform was soaked, and I was becoming aware of the straps of my equipment gouging into my skin. There was just enough light to see, and I kept glancing to the right and left to keep my position in the long, straggling skirmish line. As the sun rose to my left, the outline of Canal Eight was becoming more and more distinct, and I knew this meant that the enemy could probably see us too.

We were only about one hundred meters away from our objective when we came to a large dike approximately a meter tall that ran parallel to the canal. We crouched behind this in the cool water, making last-minute adjustments to weapons and equipment, and waited as the sky grew lighter and lighter. The CIDG platoon leader was still next to me on my right, and a little farther down the line I could make out Dan and Norm. Sweat dripped from my nose and some sort of insect buzzed around my ears. I began to hear occasional sounds of movement from the tree line to our front, and a thin trail of smoke curled from one of the huts.

Farmers rise early, I thought to myself, and was just starting to worry that we'd waited too long when I saw a squad on our western flank splashing through the paddy at a trot toward the canal. Their goal was to seal off that end of the canal to keep the enemy from getting back to their sanctuary in the U Minh. It was still very quiet, and I thought they might make it undetected. As soon as the first few men disappeared into a large growth of elephant grass at the edge of the canal, however, the silence was ripped by the *crump* of a grenade. I just had time to notice the dark smoke of the grenade rising from the high grass, then shit hit the fan.

An excited yell and a burst of submachine-gun fire erupted from the elephant grass. This was quickly answered by more shooting and the explosions of two more grenades in quick succession. *Pop-bam-crack!* Now there were shots from all along the tree line in front of us, as we were also spotted and taken under fire.

Our men immediately returned fire and the once peaceful morning was filled with the roar of machine guns, BARs, submachine guns, and rifles. I spotted the muzzle flash of a VC directly to my front. "Hell, easy shot," I whispered to myself, and extended the carbine's stock to the open position. I made sure I had it on semiauto, got into a good, solid firing position, and squeezed off my first round in combat. The satisfying crack of the little weapon was followed immediately by a *clunk* as the weapon failed to feed.

I glanced down and saw that one of the .30-cal. rounds was wedged sideways in the breech. Shit! I dropped the magazine, cleared the cartridge, reinserted the same magazine, and attempted to jack in a new round. There was a gritty sound as the silt-filled magazine again refused to feed properly.

I cursed myself for being so incompetent. My dip in the canal had caused this, and instead of sitting with my thumb up my ass and watching the sunrise, I should have been paying more attention to my rifle. I thought to myself that it was lucky it hadn't happened when I was face-to-face with Charlie. By the time I'd reloaded with a clean magazine, my easy target was long gone, but I found another likely enemy location and burned off ten or twelve quick shots.

All up and down the dike our men were still firing like mad. Their rounds, however, were going everywhere except into the enemy positions. Geysers of rice paddy water flew into the air fifty or sixty feet in front of us, and tracers sailed ten feet above the palm trees along the canal bank. Their lack of marksmanship embarrassed me. I looked down the line and caught Dan's eye. He just sadly shook his head.

My new friend, the platoon leader, was walking up and down behind our line, exhorting his troops to shoot better. He carried his carbine in his left hand, and in his right he held a three-foot length of bamboo. Our platoon's A-6 machine-gun section was nearby, ineffectively blazing away, and when the platoon leader saw this, he ran to them screaming in Vietnamese and gave them several whacks with his stick.

I got a sudden idea, and replaced the magazine in my carbine with the one filled with tracer ammo. I found a good target area where a lot of enemy fire seemed to be originating from and fired three or four evenly spaced rounds into it. I looked over at the platoon leader, caught his attention, then fired a couple of more tracers into the tree line. He caught on, told the machine-gun crew to watch my tracers, and I methodically pumped the rest of the magazine into the target. Following my example, the excited A-6 gunner calmed down and began putting some effective fire into the same area. "Number one!" the platoon leader yelled at me, his gold teeth flashing in the morning sun.

It was time to begin the assault, and Norm and Dan tried to get Pee Hole's attention. Eventually he saw the frantic arm signals indicating that we should move forward. A few yelled commands, then we were all on our feet. With a loud shout the two platoons stepped over the protective dike and began walking toward the enemy line.

This was the first of many such walks I would eventually take in Vietnam, but I will never forget that original sensation of being in a wide-open rice paddy, completely exposed, moving toward an enemy-held tree line. The VC were still firing at us, but they didn't seem to be any better shots than our troops were. Out of the corner of my eye I saw a man go down, but I couldn't tell if he had been hit or had merely tripped. My main fear was that the VC might have the capability of bringing in mortar fire on us.

As more shots flew over and around us, I instinctively began to walk bent over at the waist, as one does when walking into a driving rain. The platoon leader was still next to me, and he indicated that I should stand erect. He was telling me that as a leader, I should appear fearless to our troops, and with some embarrassment I forced myself to walk tall.

In each platoon were several men who carried Garands equipped with grenade launchers. When we were within range, they fired off a barrage, and to my surprise, most of the grenades sailed accurately into the tree line. Immediately after the shrapnel stopped whizzing by, we broke into a run and charged across the final thirty or forty meters of open ground.

I crashed through a thicket of the tropical growth, noticed a freshly vacated enemy firing position, and breaking into a clearing, knelt panting beside a coconut tree. There was a house to my right, Canal Eight flowed directly to my front, and an empty footpath stretched along the bank. No VC in sight. It wasn't until then that I realized I'd failed to reload a new magazine after firing the tracers, and that I'd made the assault with an empty weapon.

The firing tapered off as we discovered the enemy had eluded us, and we set about establishing a defensive perimeter around the area. We set up a temporary command center in the shady front yard of a house, and while reports of casualties and after-action reports began coming in, I put up the long whip and contacted camp. Using the simple transposition code Sidney and I had agreed on, I told them our location, that we had made enemy contact, and that details would follow.

As we looked around and talked with some of the villagers, what had happened became clearer. A VC unit of about twenty men had spent the night there and had already begun moving down the trail to the west by the time our men set off the booby-trapped grenade in the elephant grass. The heaviest fighting had taken place down at that end, where the squad we sent to block the trail had run into the main force. Five or six enemy guerrillas had stayed back as a rear guard and were the ones we eventually assaulted.

We found three dead Cong, two at the western end and one who stayed as rear security. We also captured one wounded VC. Our own losses were four wounded and one killed, so we claimed we'd won, although it was a close decision.

The wounded men were brought to us in the yard of the hut, and Pitzer went to work treating first our own CIDG and then the wounded prisoner. This was the first enemy soldier I had seen up close, and I looked at him curiously. He was young and obviously well fed. His uniform consisted of shorts, a black shirt, and sandals made from tires. He wore a brown plastic sun helmet covered with a camouflage net and an American pistol belt. He'd been armed with an old French MAS 36 rifle.

The VC had been shot in the leg, and it looked pretty bad. As Dan worked on him, however, he never flinched or said a word, but only glared at us with hate-filled eyes. I wondered about his hatred of us, because I held none for him. To me he was just "the adversary," and I felt about him and the rest of the Viet Cong the same way I felt about the opposing team in a sporting event. They tried to kill us, and we tried to kill them . . . nothing personal, just part of the game.

An old woman whose front yard we had commandeered hobbled out and served us small cups of tea. Her face was deeply lined and her teeth were black from chewing betel nut, but her eyes were lively and completely unafraid. As she handed me my cup, she said something in halting French.

Pee Hole was standing nearby, waiting to interrogate the prisoner, and he laughed. "She think you French," he said. He rattled off something to her in rapid Vietnamese, and I caught the word for "American."

The old *mama-san* looked at me with new interest, then smiled and said something to Pee Hole. "She say you too young come here, fight war," he told me with a laugh. I knew my own mother back in the States would probably agree with her.

War had been a part of these villagers' lives for a long time, and each house contained a solid bunker. Like storm cellars in the American Midwest, I thought. Not all the inhabitants were as brave as the old woman, and many had to be coaxed out of hiding. A thorough search of the place turned up the usual assortment of VC flags and printed propaganda. These we confiscated, but took nothing else. Our troops and the villagers treated each other with rather exaggerated politeness, which was probably the same association the villagers had with the Viet Cong.

We didn't stay in the area too long, but soon crossed the canal and marched south through the open paddy to Canal Seven where our blocking force lay. This time we marched in several columns and walked on top of the dikes. The blocking force had seen no enemy, and war stories began to fly as our bunch of veterans linked up with these noncombatants.

We took a different route back to camp, but followed the trails along the canals. We made good time doing this, although it was risky, and were back at Tan Phu in time for lunch.

Chapter 9

As time passed, I fell into the routine of life at Tan Phu. On a typical day I'd get up at dawn and stumble into the Titis Tavern where an always cheerful Hai, a nasty-looking cigarette butt dangling from his mouth, would be fanning the fire in one of the hibachis.

"Good morning, Hai. What's for breakfast?"

"Oh, very good! Have number-one pancake," he'd say, as he did every morning. Hai's pancakes were about an inch thick, as big around as a plate, and weighed a couple of pounds each. After eating one, you felt like you'd swallowed a cannonball.

"Ugh, what else you got?"

"Have oatmeal," he'd always offer. "Milk *fini*, but you eat with water instead, still okay."

"How about ham and eggs, Hai? Maybe a nice Denver omelet with fresh cheese, tomatoes, onions, and bell peppers? Whole-wheat toast and a big glass of freshly squeezed orange juice?"

"Yes, have egg. Have goose egg, I buy this morning in village. You want?"

"Just give me some coffee, Hai."

Cross and I had begun rotating the commo duties on a daily basis. If it was my day to be the operator, I'd go outside, take a look at the sky, then send in the morning weather report. It was almost always the same: scattered clouds, light and variable winds, negative precipitation. Then I'd go back to the Tavern, where the rest of the team was gathered, and relay any messages I'd received from higher headquarters. The conversation usually went something like this:

"Any word on choppers?"

"Nope."

"Any word on the supplies we requested?"

"Nope."

"Any word on when the new team sergeant will get here?"

"Nope."

"Well, fuck the bastards!"

As we ate we'd discuss the coming day's activities and each person's duties and assignments. The team medics had begun holding a sick call each morning for the local villagers. In the afternoon they gave instruction to the CIDG and LLDB medics and to the camp nurses. Someone was always getting shot, blown apart, or otherwise wounded around Tan Phu, and there were constant plague epidemics and malaria cases to worry about too, so the medics had no problem staying busy.

The two camp demo/engineer sergeants worked on camp defenses and supply, both areas where there was always plenty to do. We had started a crash program of marksmanship training, which kept the weapons men busy, and the rest of us filled in and aided in the training effort whenever we weren't busy with our primary jobs.

On a usual day I might find myself repairing the camp's lights, assisting on the rifle range, accompanying a medical patrol, and issuing clothing and equipment. Every evening, of course, I had the sitrep to look forward to, and after the sun went down the real fun started.

After the evening meal we took turns using the two showers, then changed from the standard Army fatigue uniforms we wore during the day to our night uniforms, which we slept in. Because the danger of being overrun was greatest at night, we wore the tiger-striped CIDG uniform or black "VC pajamas" after dark. Either outfit would make us harder to distinguish from the Vietnamese if we had to activate our escape and evasion plan.

The hour or so of free time we had each evening just at twilight was always the most pleasant, peaceful part of the day. War and all, it was hard to escape the fact that Vietnam was a beautiful country, and our team would usually pull chairs out onto the open area in front of our team quarters as the sun went down, smoke, bullshit, have a cold drink, and prepare ourselves for the nightly haps.

If you enjoyed getting shot at, Tan Phu was a great place to be. During the daylight hours you were fairly safe within a radius of about one kilometer of camp, although we were often fired on even then. At night I had the suspicion that the VC were using us as training aids. Usually the attacks were aimed at the outpost line, but often the camp itself would come under an attack of some sort. Sometimes the VC would sneak within range and hose us down with automatic-weapon fire. This was nerve-racking and irritating, but not particularly deadly. As we had learned in our first week in-country at the B-team, it was the goddamn mortars we had to worry about the most.

After Cross got back from the hospital, he took over the nightly alert position in the commo bunker, and I was moved out to a bunker on the berm. I liked being outside where I could see what was going on much more than being in the confines of the commo bunker, and my new position was a critical one that covered both the bridge leading from the village to the camp, and the outside of the commo bunker. The position contained a BAR, plus a supply of grenades and hand-launched flares. It was surrounded by a good, thick dirt wall, but the overhead fortification was only one layer of sandbags. The sandbags were covered by a tin roof, however, and I figured that any incoming mortar rounds would burst on the tin and the sandbags would soak up the shrapnel.

Every night, I could count on having my sleep interrupted once by guard duty and another time by an alert or an actual attack of some sort. All of us began to hope that the nightly haps would take place while we were already awake on our guard shift, because that way we'd only have to get up once.

By the second or third week at Tan Phu, I was becoming aware of other problems we faced besides the Viet Cong. These were internal political problems, something I had never had to face before in my Army career. The first problem was that a good deal of friction was developing between our detachment and the B-team.

Part of the problem was that we felt our requests for supplies were being ignored. In fact, we thought *all* our reports were being ignored, and that the B-team members were all a bunch of lazy REMFs who worked eight hours a day, then spent the rest of the time partying in Can Tho.

We had only been at Tan Phu for two or three weeks when I learned an important lesson about how a Special Forces radio operator fits into the great game of Cover Your Ass. I'd just sent a message to the B-team asking about the status of one of our supply requests, and they had fired back a message stating they'd never received any such request from us.

Leites came unglued. "Goddamnit! Let me see your

radio log and message file for everything we've sent since we got here," he told me.

I gulped, said "Yessir," and went into the commo bunker. I had a slight problem, you see, because since we'd been at Tan Phu, I hadn't been *keeping* any log or file! To any old communicators out there, this may sound like the epitome of incompetence on my part. It might have been the height of naiveté, all right, but I was actually just doing things the way I had been taught in Special Forces communications school. All my prior training had been on how to operate a clandestine radio in a guerrilla warfare situation, and in that scenario you keep no written records of any kind because of fear of capture.

Just by luck I had kept a few scribbled copies of old messages and a piece of scratch paper with occasional notes of incoming and outgoing messages. I stuck these in a folder and hurried back to where Captain Leites, the ex–first sergeant, stood fuming and mumbling to himself about how fucked up the B-team was.

It took him only a moment to glance through what I'd handed him. His face grew redder, and I thought the top of his bald head might blow off.

"What the hell is this pan of worms!" he roared, glaring at me in disbelief.

I mumbled my excuses, but they were not accepted, and I was ordered to have a complete, typed message log and in/out file prepared and submitted in one hour. I complied, giving it the full "eyewash" treatment with bound papers clipped neatly in labeled folders. This calmed the boss down some, but he always checked the commo records closely from then on. It was a lesson learned the hard way, but I kept good files after that, and several months later this helped save my career.

Our other big problem centered on the penchant the Vietnamese had for corruption. As camp commander, and as the ranking LLDB member at Tan Phu, Major Phong was considered to be the ringleader, or at least responsible, for all the scams that were going on. Captain Leites, who was an old soldier and didn't like being taken for a sucker, also happened to be absolutely honest. Besides that, one of the main reasons for having American Special Forces personnel at the A-teams was to ensure that this sort of crap didn't flourish, and Leites intended to do a good job.

A few days after our first payday at Tan Phu, Leites and Phong had a heated discussion in Phong's office. Several days later, when the next helicopter stopped by, Major Phong departed on it, saying he'd been called to an important meeting in Saigon. A few days after that we got a message ordering Leites to report to the B-team.

We all figured this summons had something to do with the battle over supplies and thought little of it. When Leites returned from the conference, however, we found out differently. Major Phong obviously had powerful political connections, because Captain Leites had been relieved of duty and would be returning to the States immediately!

Leites told us he'd been assured that this was strictly a political decision and would in no way impact his future career. None of us really believed this and figured Leites and the entire team had been given the royal shaft.

Captain Leites's departure left us without both a team sergeant and team commander. We were getting used to being shorthanded around Tan Phu, but the shoddy treatment Leites had received didn't do a whole lot for team morale. Shortly after Leites left, however, we got word that a new team sergeant, Master Sergeant Dennis Lima, was on the way.

We were all glad to hear that it was Lima, because he was well-known and liked by everyone on the team. As a very young soldier, Lima had gone to the Korean War in one of the first increments and was promoted from the rank of PFC to M.Sgt. in two years. Unlike many men who'd received fast promotion because of the war, Lima had managed to hang on to his stripes, and by the early sixties had over ten years time-in-grade. Lima had the reputation of being quite humorous, and if there was one thing we needed around Tan Phu just then, it was something to make us laugh.

It took only a couple of weeks for the powers that be to have a replacement on the way for Leites too. His name was Phil Arsenault, and no one knew much about him other than that he was ex-enlisted, had played football, and had graduated Ranger school. By the first of September both men had arrived and we were finally completely back to a full team.

It was just about this time that Bill Martin and I got the good news that we'd been promoted. Bill progressed up to Spec Four, the rank he had held more than a year before, and I made buck sergeant. We held a small ceremony out in front of the team house, with Rowe reading the orders and Arsenault stapling the new ranks onto our sleeves. I was really happy to make sergeant, because it meant that when I got back to Bragg, I'd be able to get into the NCO club, and that I wouldn't have to pull KP anymore.

Special Forces A-teams in Vietnam were on per diem, i.e., receiving a monetary allowance in lieu of rations, so we purchased all of our own food, either from the local economy or from the Navy commissary in Saigon. Like most other A-teams in Vietnam at the time, we rotated one or two men into Saigon for a few days as often as we could. The official reason for these trips was to coordinate supply requests with headquarters and to purchase commissary and PX items for the team.

The unofficial reason was R&R, which most of us assumed stood for "rape and rampage." We had a policy at Tan Phu of keeping a low profile with the locals. This meant no sexual relations of any kind while in the vicinity of the camp and no heavy drinking. No one really wanted to get drunk around camp anyway, because you needed your wits about you to survive. The ban on sex was easy too, at first, because the average local peasant woman wasn't very attractive. We had three female nurses working in the dispensary, all of them strictly dog meat, and the surest indicator of when you needed a trip to Saigon was when these hags started looking good.

Right after I got promoted, my turn to go to Saigon rolled around, and by then the nurses were looking like sex goddesses. Bill Martin was due to go in too, and it was decided we could go together. This took a lot of faith on someone's part, because Bill and I had much-deserved reputations for being the two biggest fuckups on the team. We got in enough trouble when we were both on our own, but as a pair we were strictly "a delinquency report getting ready to happen," as Lima once called us.

Captain Arsenault hadn't been there very long and didn't know Bill and me well yet, but Lieutenant Rowe sure did. I think it was his okay that finally got us the trip, and we had to personally swear to him that we wouldn't foul up. We'd have sworn to anything by that time, of course, and with our AWOL bags packed and ready, Bill and I eagerly awaited the next chopper.

Chapter 10

I'll never forget that first trip to Saigon. Bill Martin and I went from Tan Phu to Can Tho by helicopter, then hitched a ride on a Caribou. I'd been out in the rice paddy supervising a barbed-wire detail when the choppers suddenly arrived. Having been given no time to change clothes, I was covered from the waist down in dried mud. Anytime we flew anywhere in Vietnam, we wore full combat gear just in case we crash-landed, so besides carrying carbines, Bill and I were also festooned with knives, ammo, and grenades. It was late afternoon by the time we finally landed at Tan Son Nhut.

"What are we supposed to do with this shit?" I asked Bill, indicating our weapons and equipment.

"Fuck it, we'll take it with us," Bill said, and with that we simply walked over to the civilian air terminal and climbed into a cab. Our team kept a room rented at a place called the Annex for any members who happened to be in town, and as the cabbie bluffed his way through the evening traffic, I sat back and looked things over in this town I'd heard so much about.

It was love at first sight. Saigon was still "the Paris of the Orient" then. By Asian standards it was a rather quiet city with tree-lined boulevards, sidewalk cafés, and tile-roofed villas. The French had been gone less than ten years, and the place still had a colonial atmosphere.

When the driver let us out at the address we'd given him, he didn't argue over the number of piasters we handed him. Either we'd given him far too much or he was intimidated by our carbines and general unsavory appearance. We were on the sidewalk in front of a seedy-looking, four-story pink building. Following the instructions we'd been given, we entered an unmarked door and walked through a dirty passageway to the courtyard, which was actually the front of the place. Our room was on the third floor, and we reached it by way of steep stairs leading to an open walkway, like an American motel.

It was a typical, inexpensive Vietnamese apartment, consisting of one room and a Vietnamese-style bath. There were two hard, indigenous beds, each covered by a mosquito net. The bath had a squat-type crapper, a big jug of water, and a drain in the floor for bathing. A cheap wooden wardrobe for clothing stood in one corner. We threw open the louvered shutters, secured our carbines and web gear by tossing the stuff into the wardrobe, and looked at each other, grinning. Hell, after Tan Phu this place was better than the Hilton!

A smiling lackey materialized at our still-open door. "You want ice, something drink, food, women?" he asked. Christ, how did he know?

We settled for two iced La Rue beers, and as we sat on the beds savoring all the luxury, the woman situation started taking care of itself. Several of our neighbors on that floor dropped in on us to say hello and to welcome us to our visit. They were all young working girls, most of them employed as bar girls in various joints around town. None of them worked in places frequented by Americans, and they were very interested in finding out about us. Bill and I soon figured out that we were the only male tenants in the entire apartment building. I don't know who was responsible for selecting the Annex for our team safe house, but they should have been given a medal!

We had three days ahead of us. The chores of shopping at the PX and commissary would take only about half a day, so that left us with sixty-six hours to fill with as much entertainment as we could cram in. Our only worry was that an early curfew might be slapped on the city, something that would really cramp our style.

All that summer, Saigon had been in turmoil. The first Buddhist monk had burned himself in protest on the eleventh of June. Several others had followed his example in the weeks that followed, and there was rioting. Diem and his brother, Nhu, had reacted harshly to these demonstrations, with Nhu using his Vietnamese Special Forces to crush the dissenters. Only about a week before Bill and I arrived for our R&R, Nhu's men had staged midnight raids on several Buddhist pagodas, and tension was high.

Diem's sister-in-law, Madame Nhu, was very vocal in her disdain for the demonstrators. She and her husband, both Catholics, had labeled the Buddhists as being part of the communist plot. The Dragon Lady, as she was known, held a news conference and said she was delighted the monks were performing these "barbecues" and that she would gladly furnish the matches for the next one.

In the American Special Forces community, we held little sympathy for the Buddhists. There was enough to worry about in Vietnam without a bunch of religious fanatics causing more trouble, and although we realized that Nhu's heavy-handed approach was only likely to make the situation worse, most of us went along with what the Dragon Lady said about offering them matches. There were many crude jokes making the rounds, such as the one about new robes being developed for the Buddhists by DuPont. "The robes are made out of spun napalm and have a fuse lighter attached," is how the punch line of that one went.

Personally, I thought both Nhu and his wife were cool. Anyway, I had sort of a crush on the Dragon Lady. Hell, she was beautiful, rich, intelligent, powerful, ruthless, and vaguely sinister. What else could you ask for in a woman? Sure, she'd banned dancing in Saigon, but I didn't much like dancing either.

Bill and I were both exhausted, but decided we needed to check out Tu Do Street before it got much later. We hustled the giggling group of young women out of the room, cleaned up, and changed into civies. The lights were just starting to come on around the city when we walked down to the street and found a taxi.

We had the driver let us out in front of the Caravelle Hotel, and we made our way slowly down Tu Do. Known by the French as Rue Catinat, Tu Do Street was still a lovely place in '63. It was lined with first-class shops, cafés, bars, nightclubs, and restaurants, and none of them were very crowded. There weren't many Americans in-country yet, and the other round-eyed people you ran into were as likely to be European tourists as GIs.

We'd been told that the Sporting Bar, down the street at number 61, was the Special Forces hangout in Saigon, and after stopping at several other interesting joints, Bill and I eventually came to it. The Sporting Bar didn't look much different from any of the other bars on Tu Do, except it was maybe a little sleazier. There were some guys we knew from Bragg there, however, and some other guys from the 1st Group on Okinawa whom we didn't know. We were also introduced to a couple of Navy SEALs who often hung out at the Sporting.

It was quiet in the place that night, and we had a peaceful time playing liar's dice and looking over the selection of bar girls. Things were pretty straitlaced in those early days. The girls all stayed behind the bar, and although they would ask you to buy them the infamous "Saigon tea," this paid for nothing more than their company for the time it took them to sip their drink. No physical contact was allowed, not even holding hands across the bar. The girls would talk to you all night, of course, as long as you continued to buy them the expensive, fake drinks; and if they liked you, and if you could afford them, you could usually make a deal with the bar *mama-san* to buy them out at closing time. There were often other "tips" required after that, although sometimes not. In those early days of the war the situation wasn't as crassly commercial as it later became.

One thing was for certain—the girls working the bars and clubs on Tu Do were quite lovely and of a high quality. Most of them spoke fairly good English and French, and you could be pretty much assured that they were free of disease.

Bill and I bought a few Saigon teas that evening but didn't seriously pursue any of the little cuties. We went over to the Peacock Restaurant after a while and got an excellent meal of steak and french fried potatoes, then wandered around to a few more bars until everything closed at eleven. Curfew began at midnight, and everyone had to be off the streets by then.

We'd been socking down the booze all evening, and by the time we got back to our room at the Annex, we

were ready for nothing but a sound night's sleep uninter-
rupted by guard duty or incoming mortar rounds. Our
neighbors in the apartment building had also just arrived
home from their night's work, however, and they all had
different plans. As far as they were concerned, it was
time to party!

A steady stream of the young women began drifting in
and out of our room. The smiling lackey, who evidently
never slept, made trip after trip delivering bottles of Ba
Muoi Ba beer, buckets of ice, and various servings of
unrecognizable but delicious Vietnamese food. There
were girls everywhere, and as soon as one left, a new one
would crowd into the room to take her place. Bill and I
had forgotten about being tired by this time, and the fun
and games continued on into the wee hours. . . .

When I awoke the next morning to the sounds of
traffic in the street below, sunlight streamed through our
still-open windows. I was grievously wounded, a Viet
Cong evidently having sneaked in and buried an ax in the
middle of my forehead. I fearfully reached up with a
hand to inspect the wound, expecting to find blood and
brains leaking down my face. I found nothing but
smooth, unbroken flesh, and only then realized I was
simply suffering from a Ba Muoi Ba hangover. Ba Muoi
Ba, or 33, beer was said to be made with formaldehyde,
and now I could see where the rumor came from.

I distinctly remembered going to bed with one of the
little girls of the night before, but was glad to see that she
had departed already. In the other bed, Bill groaned, sat
up, and reached for a cigarette.

"Oh God, where are we?" he asked.

"Last night I thought it was heaven, but now I think it
must be hell," I told him, staggering into the bath to retch

a few times. "Do you know what time it is?" I asked him when I came out. "I think I gave my watch away last night."

"We need to get the commissary stuff done this morning," Bill said, checking the time for us, "but it's only eight . . . do you think a beer would make us feel better?"

"Probably, if I can hold it down," I told him. "I brought some Darvon, want one?"

After brushing our teeth and puking a few more times, we took the Darvon and split the remaining bottle of lukewarm beer. We started to perk up almost immediately and decided to have breakfast at one of the open-air cafés on Tu Do. On our way to the street, we saw none of the other revelers from the night before, but from many of the closed doors we heard sounds of happy snoring.

It was a pleasant, clear morning in Saigon, and things seemed peaceful enough. On all the major intersections, however, armed troops were stationed. They were in full battle gear, wearing steel helmets, flak vests, and the distinctive camouflage uniform of the LLDB.

"Looks like they expect some more trouble," I told Bill as the cab let us off once again on Tu Do.

"Yeah," he said. "Hope nothing really big breaks out until we're safely back at Tan Phu!"

We pulled up chairs at a sidewalk café that occupied a corner location. It was an inviting target for terrorists and had been bombed several times while the French were there. This, however, only made it a more interesting place for us to sit, read the English-language newspaper, and watch the morning activity around us. The coffee was excellent, and the French pastry was delicious.

I always enjoyed reading the newspaper in Saigon. The editors didn't have a real firm grasp of the English language, and sometimes made very amusing mistakes. That morning I ran across the following little story, which I read out loud to Bill.

SAIGON—Last night an American military man was attacked in an alley near Tu Do Street. He was robbed and stabbed several times. The man was rushed to a nearby hospital where his condition was listed as hopeless.

Bill laughed. "Hey, that's really telling it like it is. Do you think they really meant to say 'hopeful,' or did they mean what they said?"

By the time we'd finished our coffee and rolls and washed it all down with a few more beers, we were feeling completely revived.

"What time is it?" I asked after glancing down at my naked wrist for the hundredth time.

"It's almost ten-thirty," Bill said. "Would you please buy another watch while we're at the PX?"

"Yeah, and I suppose we ought to be getting over there now and get the chores done before we have more beer and decide to blow it off." I paused a moment as we watched two beautiful girls go floating past, their pastel-colored *au dais* fluttering in the morning breeze. "Remember," I added, "we promised Rowe we'd be good."

Filling the commissary orders was the most difficult and time-consuming of our jobs, so we decided to do that first to get it over with. We had a long list of staples to get, which consisted of items we were unable to purchase in Tan Phu village. We bought many canned goods, such as Spam, vegetables, and milk. It was difficult to transport fresh food like meat, butter, and chicken eggs back without it spoiling, but we'd discovered a place at Tan

Son Nhut where we could store it in a freezer, then pick it up at the last minute for the ride to Can Tho, where it was immediately transferred to the B-team's freezer. Once the perishables finally got to Tan Phu, they had to be consumed quickly, because our old kerosene refrigerator never really kept anything very cold.

After we had filled our large order and charging it all to our team account, the food then had to be transported out to the storage facility at the airport. This involved borrowing a truck from somewhere, loading all the stuff onto it, driving the damned thing there, unloading it all, then returning the truck. We were lucky that day and ended up with not only a truck but a Vietnamese driver and labor detail to do the work. Bill told me he'd take care of hauling the load to Tan Son Nhut by himself, and said he'd meet me at the Sporting Bar in a few hours. My hangover was starting to creep back, so I thankfully took him up on his gallant offer.

It was still early afternoon, and there weren't many other patrons in the Sporting, when a guy walked in who looked like a cross between a California surfer and a pirate. He wore cutoffs, a bright Hawaiian shirt, and flip-flop sandals, and had a gold hoop earring in one ear. He was carrying a parrot in a cage, which he placed next to him on the bar.

We got to talking, and I found out he was a SEAL, which didn't surprise me much considering his nautical look. He told me his name was Lee. "Most people just call me Animal," he said. Since his last name was the same as my first, it was easy for me to remember.

The Navy SEALs were a fairly new unit in '63, and I asked him what the difference between them and UDT was. He told me that the old UDT units had performed strictly underwater missions, but that this new unit also worked on land and were also parachutists. It was considered bad manners in our circle to ask specific questions about what a person was doing because so much of it was classified, but Lee gave me a general idea of the kinds of things SEAL teams were up to. It sounded neat. Animal Lee was an interesting character, to say the least, and although I didn't know it at the time, I'd be running into him several more times during the course of the war.

I wandered up the street and around the corner to the Morning Star Bar, where I'd been told I might find some more of the guys. The place was almost empty, and there was no one I knew, but I sat at the bar and ordered a drink anyway. I was sitting there "just minding my own business," as they say, when the trouble started.

Three garret troopers came in and sat at the bar next to me. I could tell what they were because they had that pale, pudgy, out-of-shape look that all the rear-echelon types had. They were loud and obnoxious and were talking about how rough they had it in the warehouse they worked in. Somehow I came to their attention. Maybe they got mad because I wouldn't talk to them, I don't know, but pretty soon it became obvious that they were planning to kick my skinny little ass.

You have to understand that although there were three of them, and they each outweighed me by about a hundred pounds, I wasn't particularly worried that they might physically hurt me. Hell, for the last six weeks people had been trying to kill me with mortars, machine guns, and grenades—what could three guys do to me with just their bare hands? Besides, with that typical naiveté of youth, I figured to win the fight anyway.

What I *was* worried about was getting in trouble. I'd

given my word to Rowe and the rest of the team, and I certainly didn't want to spend my only two remaining days of R&R in some Saigon jail. On the other hand, the thought of letting these assholes push me around was unthinkable too. I was in one hell of a bad situation.

By this time the three of them, wearing evil smiles of anticipation, had moved over to where I sat at the bar and stood around me in a semicircle. Just then four fellows I knew from Bragg came walking through the bar door, and was I ever glad to see them. I couldn't have asked for a better bunch of reinforcements to arrive, because all four were monsters, the kind of guys who liked to eat glass and bust beer bottles over one another's heads just for fun. They took in the situation at a glance and came strolling over to where our little scene was enacting itself.

"Hey, Wade, what's going on?" one of them asked me casually.

"Oh, nothing much," I said. "These puke, REMF, leg bastards were just telling me how they were winning the war here in Saigon for us, but I think they were getting ready to leave."

My antagonists, now outnumbered themselves, made a groveling retreat and the situation was saved . . . but it had been a close call.

After a quick nap back at the Annex, Bill and I decided to go high-class that night and really do the Tu Do Street bar scene right. We exchanged great wads of American money for piasters with a shady Vietnamese gangster in an alley, jumped into new clothes we'd just bought, and headed back to the bright lights.

We were having a few drinks at a place a couple of doors up the street from the Sporting when we were expertly roped in by a couple of young lady bartenders. Money and Saigon tea flowed like water. The girl who had homed in on me spoke pretty good English. She spoke some French too, and I found out she was ethnic Chinese.

We told each other the usual things that bar girls and soldiers always do, and I found myself enjoying her company. She was not the prettiest one, but she had a nice figure and straight, shiny black hair. It was something indefinable that hooked me, though, something about the air of authority she had and the no-nonsense way she talked to the customers and the other girls. She told me her name was Lyn and wrote it on a napkin for me. She was delighted when I told her my first name, because it was also such a common Chinese name.

When the bar closed, I made arrangements to go home with her. The building she lived in was only a couple of blocks away, and we walked there, mingling with the rest of the after-hours crowd, all of us anxious to get off the street before curfew. We ducked into a passageway, through a small courtyard, and up two flights of stairs. Her room was at the end of a hall. I saw an old card glued on the door with the name of some Air Force major on it. Lyn noticed me reading it and told me, "He old boyfriend. Go home States now."

Her apartment was nice, better than I'd expected. There was one large, spacious room with fans hanging from a high ceiling. A door led into a fairly modern bath. In the far corner stood an ornate, king-size bed with the mandatory mosquito net for a canopy. A fancy folding divider separated the sleeping area from the sitting section. There was a small refrigerator against the wall by the bath. The Air Force major had lived comfortably, I thought.

"You sit," Lyn told me, indicating the couch. She went to her refrigerator and brought me an ice-cold bottle of 33 beer. "I go change," she said, went into the bath, and closed the door. I heard water running.

The couch faced a large double window covered with the usual louvered wooden shutters. I got up, opened them, and then sat again, sipping my beer and listening as the noise in the street below slowly died away. As I waited I thought about this new, marvelous world I'd discovered and how happy I was to be there.

Lyn came back wearing black silk pajamas. We embraced, and I realized it was the first time we had touched each other all night.

She led me around the divider and pointed to a man's silk robe hanging on a hook. "You wash now," she said, motioning toward the bath.

I took a couple of steps and then stopped. I wasn't sure of the proper etiquette and felt like an idiot. "Should I pay now?" I asked her.

She looked at me for a moment without answering, then apparently made her decision. "Tomorrow you go PX?" she asked.

I nodded yes.

"Tomorrow you buy me presents PX. Tonight no money." She was smiling. "You young boy, I girlfriend. No money."

Just before dawn I woke to find Lyn on her side, head propped up on one hand, looking at me. "How old you?" she asked.

"Twenty-one," I answered.

"You young boy," she said again, as she had earlier.

"Lyn young girl. Lyn twenty-two." Then she went back to sleep.

When I woke up again it was late morning, and Lyn was already dressed and putting on her makeup. She had some errands to run; I didn't understand what they were. She asked me to get her some American toothpaste and soap and a bottle of scotch from the PX.

"Your friend, he look for you already," Lyn told me.

I asked where he was, and she told me he was in a room downstairs. I asked her what time it was.

"Why you no have watch?" she said crossly, and I told her I'd broken it.

"You come back tonight?" she asked. When I told her I would, she told me I could stay in her apartment as long as I liked that morning. When I left, she said, the land-lady would lock the door. She gave me a sisterly peck on the cheek, said she would see me later at the bar, and hur-ried out.

Later that day Bill and I went to the PX and bought all the items on our long list, and I bought a new Timex watch too. On the way out a plainclothes CID agent stopped us, identified himself, and asked us why we'd purchased so much stuff. We explained that we were buying for an entire A-team, and he let us go with no fur-ther protest—of course, we didn't tell him that half the crap was for our new girlfriends!

I stayed with Lyn that night too, and then it was time to return to camp. "Anytime you come Saigon, you can stay my place," Lyn told me. I told her I didn't know when or if I'd ever get back, but thanked her. I had no idea at the time, of course, that I'd be taking her up on this offer on a number of occasions during the course of the next eight years.

Chapter 11

I returned from Saigon hungover and more exhausted than when I left, but mentally refreshed. The camp nurses were ugly again, my libido was back in its cage, and I was ready to resume fighting the war.

After a rocky first six weeks, things at Tan Phu seemed to be running smoother. Our detachment was up to full strength for the first time since we arrived, recruiting of new strikers was going great guns, our training efforts were having some positive effect, and the supply problems seemed to have been resolved.

Major Phong returned to camp after an absence of several weeks. I'm sure he wanted to let the heat die down after his power struggle with Leites. All of us on the team resented Phong for getting Leites relieved, but at the same time we liked having him in camp. He might have been a crook, a political back-stabber, and all of that, but we also appreciated his combat experience and his first-hand knowledge of the enemy we faced.

Like every other A-team in Vietnam, we had our problems with the LLDB. Several of the LLDB at Tan Phu were incompetent and worthless, but we also had some pretty good ones. Throughout the course of the war the U.S. constantly faulted the Vietnamese soldiers for lack of aggression and downright cowardice. What we failed to take into consideration was that they were in for the long haul, and we were there only for a few months or years. Many of the Vietnamese had already been fighting for over fifteen years by the time we got over there, and they had nothing to look forward to but more of the same. The Vietnamese had their quota of heroes and aggressive go-getters, but such guys tended to get killed quickly, leaving only the more cautious survivor types to continue fighting the war.

Our new team sergeant, Lima, was living up to his reputation as a stand-up comedian, and he was immediately accepted by the team. Captain Arsenault was having more difficulty fitting in. A lot of this was due to this aggressive "hooha-hooha" Ranger school style of leadership. Special Forces always preferred to use finesse, cleverness, cunning, and stealth whenever possible rather than the "fix bayonets and charge" approach of other infantry units, and Arsenault's attitude and personality definitely fell into the latter category.

Of course, it's very difficult when any new commander comes in to take over a team. Our detachment had been together for quite a while and already had been through some combat together. Captain Arsenault was the outsider. There was also friction between Captain Arsenault and Lieutenant Rowe, although both tried in a professional manner to minimize it. Rowe was very well liked by all of us, was with the team from the beginning, and had done a great job as acting detachment commander while we waited for a replacement for Leites to get there. There was also the fact that Lieutenant Rowe was a West Point graduate, something that apparently grated on a newly-up-from-the-ranks officer like Arsenault.

We were constantly attempting to expand our sphere of control in the AO, and our troop levels had increased enough to allow establishment of a strongpoint outside our usual outpost line. The area we picked for this was about two kilometers east of camp along the northern bank of the major canal that ran to the town of Cho Hoi. There had been numerous reports from our agents in the area of increased VC activity, and we hoped to make it more difficult for them.

The position was within range of not only our camp mortars, but of the 155s at Thoi Binh. We put some of our best, most experienced men out there, and they spent time building well-fortified positions. Altogether, the strongpoint was manned by a reinforced platoon consisting of about forty-five men, and my pal, the CIDG platoon leader with the gold teeth, was in command. I made several trips to the position to help them with various commo problems and to show them how to build jungle antennas for their radios. I felt pretty damned isolated out there even during the day and knew that it must be a really spooky place at night.

Lieutenant Rowe made several trips down the canal to the artillery unit at Thoi Binh and was successful in his efforts at improving their accuracy. The 155 gunners had a supply of rounds with VT fuses that could be adjusted to get airbursts at ten or fifteen feet above ground. A 155 round bursting in the air over infantry troops in an open rice paddy was extremely lethal. It took a few weeks to train the crews on how to properly adjust the projectile, though, because at first many of their airbursts went off so far above the ground that they resembled anti-aircraft fire.

Our new strongpoint had direct communications both

with the guns at Thoi Binh and with our mortars. There were several minor probes of the position immediately after it was established, and the camp fired illumination in support. A couple of weeks passed during which the outpost killed a few VC and brought in several prisoners. Intelligence reports indicated that the outpost was in the tactical area of the VC 306th Battalion, and that the unit was bragging they would soon wipe it out. Secretly I suspected that was exactly what would happen, but Major Phong was confident the unit could defend itself. As it turned out, Phong was correct, and the night the 306th attempted to overrun our outpost became our major victory at Tan Phu.

We had ample warning that something was going to happen. That afternoon at 1400 hours, Phong came over to our operations center with Pee Hole.

"Tonight, VC attack outpost," Phong said.

This was typically how we got the word on such things, and our questions about exactly where the info came from were always answered with vague references to Major Phong's private intelligence network. After the first few weeks at Tan Phu, we'd discovered that Phong's secret agent reports were generally reliable, and we stopped trying to find out any more about his sources.

We sent a boat down the canal to the outpost with more ammunition, spare batteries for the PRC-10s, and a few more men. The CIDG platoon leader was briefed on the situation and told to have his shit in order as soon as the sun went down.

Back at camp, Ponce and Lowe fired a few rounds from our 81mm mortar to make sure they were registered on all the likely avenues of approach and retreat, and on any areas the weapons of the outpost couldn't cover.

Carey and Martin made sure both our 81 mortar and the one controlled by the LLDB had a good supply of HE and illumination. Phong sent another boat patrol down to Thoi Binh to brief the district chief about what to expect. After that we simply waited for the sun to go down.

As soon as it got dark, the camp went on full alert. I went to my bunker on the berm and Cross went to the commo bunker. We had already sent the B-detachment a short message that afternoon warning them that we expected trouble, and Cross made another commo check to make sure we still had good commo with them. Lowe and Ponce manned the mortar, Van and Pitzer got ready to start receiving casualties, Carey and Martin were prepared to issue more ammo, and the command element roamed around waiting for the show to begin.

We didn't have long to wait at all. At about 2200 hours the attack got under way. The trouble was, the VC were smarter than we thought. Their first attack wasn't against the eastern strongpoint, but directed at us in camp. It came from the vicinity of the outpost line, which was on the other side of the village to our west.

The men at the outpost heard or saw something and fired a round of illumination from their 60mm mortar. As soon as it lit up the area, there was a long burst of machine-gun fire. The noise of the machine gun covered up the sound of the VC mortars firing, and the next thing we knew the inside of our camp perimeter erupted as round after round impacted, filling the night with fire and shrapnel.

The VC gunners were damned good, because every one of their rounds landed inside the camp. The VC fired all the rounds in a period of about fifteen seconds, and they landed with the effect of a "time on target" barrage.

Had we all been rushing to our alert positions as we normally would have, instead of being already under cover, the results would have been much worse than they were.

The man on duty in our tower had a clear shot over the village and had seen the flashes as the VC rounds left the tubes. He got the .30 Browning cooking, and tracers laced through the air. The outpost line had also come under attack, and they opened up with everything they had.

It seemed for a few minutes that we might expect a major ground attack from the west. If the enemy got through the thinly manned outpost line, their movement would be screened on that side of camp by the village. The main canal lay between camp and the village, though, so we were pretty safe from that direction unless they attempted a direct assault in force across the bridge . . . and my bunker was directly in front of it.

All this passed through my mind in much less time than it takes to say it. I pulled the cocking handle of the BAR back, then slid it forward again to lock it in place, tapped up on the magazine a couple of times, and got lined up so I aimed down the middle of the dimly lighted bridge. I made a quick inventory of ammo and saw that I had about twenty loaded magazines. The BAR was a weapon I liked, and I was confident in my ability to bring some real smoke if a horde of the bastards tried to get across, but I wished I had something even better. A quad .50 would have been great!

I heard the sound of running footsteps behind me, and Captain Arsenault ducked through the bunker entrance. He was carrying a 3.5" rocket launcher and a couple of HE rounds.

"Do you know how to use this thing?" he asked, catching his breath.

"Sure," I told him, trying not to take my eyes off the bridge.

"If they start to come across, try to blow the bridge with this," he told me. "I know it won't do much good, but it's all I could find."

The reason it wouldn't do much good, of course, is that the 3.5" rocket was designed to knock out tanks and contained a shaped charge that would do little more than punch a hole in the wooden bridge.

He stayed with me a moment or two longer, and we looked across the canal at the still-peaceful village. "You should have plenty of warning if they try to come this way," he said. "They'll have to fight their way through the platoon we have stationed over there, and they're dug in on the far edge of the village."

I told him I was counting on that and asked him if anyone had been hit by the incoming mortar rounds. "Two or three strikers were wounded, one of them pretty bad," he said. "Carey picked up a piece of frag in the back."

"Will we need to call in a medevac?" I asked.

"No, Pitzer looked at him and said he'd be okay," the captain told me. "Give a yell if you need anything," he said, then hurried out. Arsenault was really in his element in this kind of situation, and I realized that although this was probably the most combat he'd seen so far, he appeared to have everything under control.

No ground assault developed from the west, and it soon became apparent that all the VC activity so far had been simply a feint to draw our attention away from our strongpoint, which was still their real objective. Had we not had good intelligence of their true intentions, the enemy might have been more successful.

Suddenly the sky over the eastern strongpoint lit up with the glow of trip flares and illumination rounds from their 60 mortar. Two or three tracers ricocheted high into the air. A few moments later the sound of the battle reached us, and we heard the muffled *crump* of claymores and grenades intermingled with the crackle of small-arms fire.

Our camp mortars and the 155s began firing in support almost without hesitation, because they had wisely remained focused on the concentrations around the strongpoint instead of shifting their aim to the other direction, as the VC had hoped. The whooshing sound of the big 155 rounds was quite audible as they lumbered on their way overhead toward their objective. I thought about what it would be like getting caught in the middle of a rice paddy, knee deep in water, with nothing between me and an airbursting 155 but a plastic helmet! Maybe this will teach the fuckers, I thought.

Things raged hot and heavy for several hours. The small force attacking the camp tried to keep us occupied to relieve the pressure we were putting on their comrades to the east, and the guns at Thoi Binh also came under sporadic fire. None of it had much effect, however, and we continued to lob round after round of indirect fire in support of the beleaguered strongpoint. As is usual in these situations, the excited radio reports we received were only semicoherent, but it appeared that our strikers were not only holding out, but winning.

By the time the first streaks of light began to show in the east, the battle had about run its course, and by sunrise it was all over. We put together a patrol of several platoons to go check out the area, and I accompanied it, anxious to see the gory results of our night's work.

I expected to see a battlefield covered with bodies, but there were only a few. The VC were noted for being very meticulous at policing a battlefield, however, and the fact that we found anything at all was a sign that they'd been hurt badly. Besides the bodies, we captured a couple of wounded who had been left behind. There were many blood trails, lots of discarded equipment, and even several weapons. As we checked around the perimeter, I came upon a couple of our strikers laughing and tossing something back and forth. I thought at first they were playing with a snake, but when I got closer I saw they'd found part of a VC foot.

My buddy, the CIDG platoon leader, was jubilant as he recounted the battle to me in broken English.

"They come here first," he said, pointing to the wire that marked his northern perimeter, "we shoot claymore, *boom!* We shoot machine gun, *bang-bang-bang!* We kill too many!" He pantomimed a VC grabbing his chest and falling dead. "Then we call mortar and 155, *boom-boom!*" he said, excitedly trying to imitate the sound of the artillery. "Oh, is number one! VC try retreat over there," he said, pointing to a small grove of trees that had been almost completely defoliated by bursting shells. "I tell camp shoot mortar. . . ." He rattled on and on, radiant in his victory.

Our men at the strongpoint had suffered only three wounded and none killed. After scouting around the area and finding no more signs of the enemy, we radioed camp and had them send a couple of our boats to take back the casualties. One of the wounded VC had died while Pee Hole attempted to interrogate him, and we dumped his body, along with the others, in the canal.

"Fish like eat, think number one chop-chop," the platoon leader said, leering as the bodies drifted away in the slow current. There were many large catfish in the canals, and I made a mental note not to eat any more of the ones we purchased locally at the Tan Phu market.

After several days, intelligence reports began to come into camp confirming that we had indeed mauled the enemy badly. As far as could be determined, we had killed about fifty of them, mostly with the artillery, and wounded many more. The commander of the VC 306th Battalion had taken it all personally and was vowing revenge. His threats didn't bother us much, as we had just kicked some major butt and were full of confidence. A month or so later we would be wishing we'd taken the warning more seriously.

Team medic VandeBerg in Tan Phu village checking out a couple of dead Viet Cong. Camp Tan Phu is in the background.

The author operating the ANGRC-109 radio in the commo bunker. Strictly low-tech in those days: I'm using a Morse code leg key.

The author and his Model 97 riot gun getting ready to go on the "mound-demolition project" described in chapter 23.

The author and his squad leader buddy, called Gold Tooth in the book. Photo taken in the photography shop at Tan Phu village.

The author's promotion to buck sergeant. Left to right: Nick Rowe (holding orders), the author, and Arsenault (stapling on my stripes).

Some of our typical troops at Tan Phu. Many of these guys were killed during the big battle of October 29.

View from machine-gun position at south end of camp. Weapon is a Browning 1919 .30 caliber, air-cooled machine gun.

(above) Several weeks after A-23 returned to Fort Bragg from Vietnam, we are on the rifle range firing foreign weapons. Left to right: Cross, Martin, Lowe, the author, VandeBerg, Shipley (who had replaced Pitzer), Carey, Browning, Arsenault, Navarro, and Lima. (Courtesy of Bill Martin)

(right) Good photo of Nick Rowe with our snake, Harvey. The cook, Hai, can be seen in the background. (Courtesy of Bill Martin)

(above) Bill Martin standing with two CIDG company
commanders. They had just returned from an operation.
(Courtesy of Bill Martin)

(below) Rowe talking with Tinh (the acting camp commander
during Phong's absence) a few days before Rowe was captured.
(Courtesy of Bill Martin)

(left) John Lowe giving marksmanship classes. (Courtesy of Bill Martin)

(below) Standing in front of our operations center. Left to right: Martin, Lima, CIDG company commander, and unknown striker. (Courtesy of Bill Martin)

"Barracks rats" at Fort Bragg. A noontime card game is in progress. Left to right: VandeBerg, Cross, McClure, and Smith. McClure and Smith were on our sister team, A-21, and both were captured at Hiep Hoa. Smith was the owner of the infamous "Big E." (Courtesy of Bill Martin)

(left) Pluto, our team dog.
(Courtesy of Bill Martin)

(below) Photo taken of camp from the tower. Dispensary is in the foreground. Behind are the thatch buildings that housed the U.S. and the Vietnamese Special Forces (LLDB) teams, the operations center, the commo bunker, and the CIDG barracks. (Courtesy of Bill Martin)

The drop zone, looking back toward the camp. A resupply has just come in, and a camouflaged parachute is in the foreground. (Courtesy of Bill Martin)

(above) The entire CIDG on parade just prior to "The Great Rocket Launch Demonstration."
(Courtesy of Bill Martin)

(below) Photo taken looking down the berm on the east side of camp. Notice moat and low dirt berm with *punji* stakes. This was all we had between us and 50 billion blood-crazed Viet Cong.
(Courtesy of Bill Martin)

(above) Left to right: Martin, the author, and Cross standing in front of the B Company, 5th Special Forces, buildings the day after we returned to Fort Bragg from Tan Phu. Bleak, cold, and depressing.
(Courtesy of Bill Martin)

(below) Bill Martin (right) and the author in 1995 at the Special Forces Association annual convention in Las Vegas.
(Courtesy of Bill Martin)

Chapter 12

". . . I don't care if it's a bicycle or a goddamned *tricycle*, if you get a DUI, you'll put it on blocks!" We were all sitting around in the Titis Tavern, howling with laughter, as Lima played us his tape-recorded impersonation of the 5th Group commander.

"So anyway," Lima said, continuing with his story, "we were all supposed to be out on police call picking up pinecones, but instead we snuck back to the team room. I've got my whole team up there, except for the officers, and we're listening to this tape. All of a sudden I hear someone yell 'Attention!' and I peek out the door, and who's standing there at the top of the fucking stairs, but Wills himself!"

Lima certainly livened things up around Tan Phu, sometimes in more ways than just telling stories. Sergeant Lima was one of those closet demo men who loved to play with explosives. He had attended an advanced demo course taught by the CIA and enjoyed showing off the many tricks he'd learned. Some of the improvised explosive devices that he, Carey, and Martin cooked up worked out pretty well, while others were downright disasters.

One of the devices that worked well was the foo-gas

projector. Foo-gas was a popular weapon for A-teams in the early sixties, and could be a very effective defensive munition, especially against mass enemy attacks coming through your wire. Foo-gas projectors were made by burying a fifty-five-gallon drum of napalm or some other sticky, flammable liquid at an angle with one end of the barrel pointed toward the area the enemy was expected to assault from. A piece of det cord was looped around the front rim of the barrel, then run to a small charge of TNT and thermite at the bottom end. When set off, the det cord cut the top off the barrel, then ran back to the TNT and thermite, which exploded and blew the flaming liquid out over a wide area, similar to a napalm bomb.

For some reason, we could never get enough claymore mines at Tan Phu, so the demo sergeants and Lima also came up with a way to build our own "super claymores." These were made out of large metal ammo cans. The bottom of the cans held a charge of C-4 molded in a concave shape, and the rest of the can was filled with old cartridge cases, the links from machine-gun belts, nails, rocks, broken glass, and anything else we could find that might mangle a human body. We placed several of these improvised claymores so they covered a danger area near the front gate and ran the firing devices back to the nearest machine-gun bunker.

Early one evening we were all sitting around the Tavern before going to bed. We weren't expecting anything to happen that early, because the Cong didn't usually start their fun and games until close to midnight. All of a sudden we heard several large explosions from the vicinity of the front gate, followed immediately by shouts and the usual wild fuselage of small-arms fire.

There was mass confusion as we scrambled for our

guns and equipment. "Kill those damned lights!" some-one yelled. In the darkness that followed, people bumped into each other, chairs tipped over, and a man cursed as he went sprawling on the floor. We finally got to our equipment and ran to our alert positions, only to discover that it had all been a false alarm.

Back in the Titis Tavern, Rowe told us what had happened. It seems there was a new CIDG guard at the front gate bunker. He'd been messing around with the "super claymore" firing device and set them off by accident. All the other troops on that end of camp thought we were under attack and opened fire.

"Oh God, they're comin' through the gate!" someone said in mock terror, referring back to the voice we'd heard the night we'd been attacked at the B-team. We found this very amusing, and from then on anytime one of us jumped at a sudden noise, which happened often due to our frayed nerves, another team member would say, "They're comin' through the gate!" or "They're comin' over the walls!" and everyone would crack up in wild laughter.

Even taking a shit was a nerve-racking event at Tan Phu. I know this sounds funny to someone who has never been in a similar situation, but if you've been there, you'll know what I mean. When we first got to Tan Phu, the crapper consisted of a small thatch outhouse set off in the middle of a cleared area. We crapped into containers made from fifty-five-gallon drums, and every few days someone would have to drag the drums out, pour diesel fuel over the stinking mess, and burn it. Even with frequent burning, the latrine was a foul-smelling, nasty place, always buzzing with flies. Because it was too damned hot to sit in the outhouse during the day, most of us tried to wait until night, when it was cooler.

Imagine yourself trying to take a shit. It's two in the morning, you're pulling your shift of guard duty, and you've been holding it all day, waiting for this chance. The privy sits invitingly out in the moonlight. Just moving around inside the camp at night is a challenge, because all the strikers are jumpy and trigger happy. You walk to the crapper, using the red filter on your flashlight not only to see where you're going, but to identify yourself to the strikers. Even so, amid the sounds of rounds being jacked into chambers and safeties clicking off, you are challenged several times before you get to your destination. "Okay, okay," you tell them, "number one."

Once at the stinking latrine, you look around nervously. It sits out alone, thirty meters from the nearest bunker or cover. You go in, leaving the door open so you won't feel so trapped, and lean your carbine in one corner. Next you take off your web gear and set it on the floor. Now the big moment comes, and you drop your camouflage trousers down around your ankles and climb up on the wooden perch. You've just let out a long sigh of relief when the first VC mortar round bursts.

I think it was Sergeant Lima who got the idea to build a new, safer latrine for exclusive use of the American team. There was an old, cement emplacement dating from the time of the French that we weren't using for anything. It sat right on the bank of the canal, not far from the American team house. The thing was cylindrical in shape, had a flat, cement roof, and was just the right size for a one-seat outhouse.

One evening around the supper table we discussed the

possibilities of converting the emplacement into a clean, fortified latrine.

"It's just the right size," someone offered.

"Yeah," Lima said, "and I've been thinking that we could rig it up with a pipe running down to the canal so we could flush it!"

There was some discussion of this idea, both pro and con, the con being the fact that we wouldn't be setting a very good example for the locals by flushing our turds into the canal they used for washing their dishes and clothes. Someone brought up the fact that all the locals were already using it for a sewer and always had, so we finally decided that the added turds of twelve Americans couldn't pollute it any more than it already was.

"Just make sure none of those yo-yo civic action people finds out about it," Pitzer added, "or there'll be hell to pay."

Lima said he didn't have anything to do the next day and would start work on the project, and because I was always looking for an excuse to get away from the radio, I volunteered to help him. The next morning we were out bright and early examining the old bunker. Lima had seen a length of four-inch pipe lying around that would just reach the edge of the canal. The first part of the project would involve punching a hole through the cement wall at the base of the bunker just large enough for the pipe to fit through.

"What I figure we can do," Lima told me, "is steal a bag of that cement we're supposed to use only for civic action projects in the village and use it to mold a toilet bowl around the end of the pipe. We'll put a seat on it and keep a bucket of water in here at all times. Then, after a person gets done, they can use the water to flush it all down through the pipe to the canal."

The wall of the bunker was only six inches thick and made out of low-grade cement that was mostly sand. It would have been a simple matter to knock a four-inch hole through the wall in minutes using a hammer or even just a screwdriver, but Lima had another plan.

"Let's do this the *easy* way," Lima said. "Ever hear of an 'earmuff' charge?" I told him I'd heard of it but didn't really know how to make one. He said he'd teach me, and we set about gathering the needed materials and putting it all together.

An earmuff charge looked just like the name implied, and consisted of two small shaped charges placed directly opposite each other on either side of a wall. The charges were looped together with a piece of det cord, and the blasting cap was situated in the exact center of this loop. When the charge was detonated, both the shaped charges went off simultaneously, firing their jets toward each other. I believe the earmuff charge was actually designed for putting neat holes in something like a very tough, thick, tempered steel wall.

The project took a lot longer than we thought, and it was the middle of the afternoon before we were ready to try it out. We'd made the little shaped charges out of C-4 and tin cans, had carefully measured everything so that the det-cord leads were exactly the same length and the shaped charges were exactly opposite each other on both sides of the wall.

Several other team members stood with us to watch how it worked. "Fire in the hole," Sergeant Lima yelled gleefully as he pulled the fuse lighter. A minute later there was a deafening roar as the thing went off. At first our new crapper was concealed from view by the big cloud of dust kicked up by the explosion, but as it cleared we were able to see the results of our day's work.

"Ummm, guess we made the shaped charges a little big," Lima said as we all walked over to take a closer look. Our earmuff charge had blown a three-foot hole in the side of the bunker, displaced the flat roof by several feet, and put two large cracks in the wall.

The next day we found a couple of Vietnamese strikers who knew about cement work, and they patched it all up. By the end of the week we were using our clean, fortified, stinkless shitter.

Something most people don't think much about when considering the possible ways to get wounded or killed in a war is accidents. Anytime you get a lot of men together and load them down with a bunch of lethal weapons and munitions, you are going to have a few accidents, no matter how hard you try to be careful.

One day we were on the range teaching a group of CIDG how to fire the 57mm recoilless rifle. We had repeatedly warned them about the danger of the back blast the weapon generated, and had performed the usual demonstration of placing a couple of boxes behind the weapon when it was fired so they could watch the back blast blow them to pieces. The danger was greatest when firing the weapon from the prone, because the gunner had to lie at an angle to keep his legs out of the back-blast area. Of course, it wasn't long before one of the troops managed to get his right leg in the way, causing a wound that looked as if he'd been hit with a shotgun.

On another occasion we had all just turned in for the night when there was a burst of automatic-weapon fire from the CIDG barracks directly behind us. You can imagine the excitement this caused in the American end of the compound, because the fear of an internal attack by VC infiltrators was always on our minds. In this case it turned out to be just another accident. A striker had returned from guard duty and tossed his fully loaded and cocked M-3 "grease gun" down on his cot. The trigger had caught on something, killing the guy in the next bed and wounding two others.

The American team wasn't immune to accidents either. The worst one we suffered was a result of another improvised munitions experiment. It happened during what I always remember as "The Great Rocket-Launch Demonstration."

Although there was no armor threat in the area, we had a large supply of 3.5 rockets at Tan Phu. One day the demo men and Lima were talking about a method of laying an anti-armor ambush using just the round itself without the launcher. This involved rigging up four or five rockets to fire electrically using a dry cell battery, then hiding them on the side of a likely avenue of approach and using a trip wire to shoot them at the target.

Lima and Martin began experimenting and found out that by firing the rockets off steel fence pickets set in the ground at different angles, the impact point of the rounds could be adjusted accurately enough to convert them into long-range, area-type weapons. Because we were always looking for other indirect-fire weapons to supplement the camp's mortars, everyone was quite enthused with this idea.

The LLDB demo man, Sergeant Van, got involved in the project too. Soon the three of them had erected several launch sites, consisting of four or five rockets each, at various critical locations around the perimeter. One of these sites was next to the bunker occupied by Sergeant Hardy and the LLDB intel sergeant, Pee Hole.

We were very proud of these "secret weapons," and one quiet evening just at sundown, hoping to avoid another incident such as the one involving the "super claymores," we decided to demonstrate our handiwork to the strikers so they would know how the rockets were to be used.

Before the demonstration, we held a formation of the entire strike force, and Major Phong briefed them on what they were about to witness. He told them to imagine the camp was under attack and that we were taking fire from a group of VC in the area the rockets were laid in on. The formation was then ordered to fall out and assemble at a safe distance behind Hardy's bunker to observe what would happen to the foolish VC attackers.

On cue, the main actors in this drama, Hardy and Pee Hole, walked to the bunker amid the wild cheers of the assembled troops. The suspense mounted as Hardy attached the leads, which were WD-1 field telephone wire, to the ten-cap blasting machine.

"Okay, Hardy," Lima yelled, "here comes the count-down: three, two, one . . . *blast off!*"

There was a loud, satisfying roar as the four rocket motors simultaneously ignited. There was an even louder noise when, after traveling only ten feet toward their target, all four of the rocket warheads exploded!

There was a moment of stunned silence as the dust and debris slowly began to settle. "What the hell . . . ?" Sergeant Lima muttered. Then Hardy came staggering out of the dust cloud, holding his shoulder. At first we all thought he was joking, because although he'd been directly under the blast, he'd also been protected by the bunker.

"I'm hit, get a medic," he yelled, and we realized it was for real.

Somehow, a piece of frag about the size of a pencil eraser had found its way through an opening in the bunker and struck Hardy in the shoulder. Although the piece wasn't very big, it was moving at a high velocity and had burrowed in deeply, ripping muscle, tendon, and bone.

It was dark when Pitzer came over to the commo bunker and told Sidney and me that he wanted to evac Hardy that night. "He's going in and out of shock, and I can't control it. It might kill him," Dan said.

This was the first time we'd asked for a medical evacuation at night, and we weren't sure if we could really even get one. The radio frequency was fairly clear, however, commo was good for a change, and the B-team reacted immediately without their usual requests for details of the situation.

About 2300 hours we heard the twin rotors of an H-21, and Bill and I lit the gasoline and sand fire pots to mark our LZ. The chopper landed on our small pad with no problem, Hardy was immediately put on board, and the helicopter departed. The whole operation took less than a minute.

As soon as it got light we held our own little board of inquiry to find out what the hell went wrong. It didn't take too long to pin the blame on the LLDB demo sergeant, Van. He had put together Hardy's launch site, and an inspection of his work on another site told the full story.

"You're supposed to attach the lead wires to the rocket

motor wires using a simple, rolling twist," Bill told us, thoroughly disgusted. "You want the wires tight enough to transmit the electricity, but loose enough so they'll pull apart easily after the motor ignites. Sergeant Van hooked the wires together using a fucking Western Union pigtail splice!" When the rockets reached the end of their tether, the resulting jerk had been enough to set them off.

A couple of days later we got a message from the B-team telling us that Norm was being evacuated back to the States. We were once again shorthanded, something that was getting to be a normal situation for us on A-23.

Chapter 13

It was in the early part of October, I believe, when higher headquarters informed us that we would be having a reporter from one of the major newsmagazines come stay with us for a while. They told us he had promised not to get in the way, and that we should just go about our normal routine.

We had mixed emotions about this upcoming visit. We were always glad to get any kind of visitors around camp, just to have someone new to talk to for a change. We had long since heard all of each other's stories, so fresh faces and viewpoints were always welcome. On the other hand, we weren't looking forward to having a non-combatant hanging around camp whom we would have to constantly baby-sit and worry about.

The B-detachment commander personally brought him out to introduce him, and we were given to believe that the visit had the full blessing and backing of "the powers that be" somewhere at the highest levels of authority back in Saigon.

The reporter, whose name I won't mention, was a small, quiet guy with a receding hairline who appeared to be in his late twenties. He was loaded down with the usual array of cameras and equipment, and began shooting photos at once. "Don't worry about me," he told us. "If I start getting to be a bother, just tell me."

He was allowed full run of the camp. Someone on the team, I forget who it was, was assigned as escort, and the reporter was given the standard VIP tour of the camp, the outposts, the village, and so on. On his second day with us he accompanied VandeBerg on one of our frequent medical patrols up the canal and seemed impressed by the number of patients and by the variety of ailments that our medics treated on a daily basis.

The local villagers, especially those near camp, were on good terms with both our CIDG troops and with our team. Even the people farther away, who were dominated by the large VC presence in the area, seemed glad to see us once they figured out we were offering medical assistance.

"I notice there's no young men around any of these villages," the reporter mentioned. "All we see is women and old people."

"Sure," VandeBerg told him, "they're all in the army. If they don't join our side, the Cong recruiters come around and take them. There's no one left to tend the rice fields but women and old men."

When our predecessors first arrived in the area to open the camp, they'd made a practice of passing out candy to the village children. This, they soon figured out, was a bad mistake, and they'd ceased the practice, but the damage had already been done. As a result, wherever Americans went in the area, we were followed by a mob of children with their hands out, begging for candy. The reporter, being a new face and considered "fresh meat" by the kids, received special attention from them.

There was a combat operation scheduled to pull out

early the next morning, and the reporter asked to go along, saying he was anxious to get some action photos. Bill, Ponce, and Dan were the other Americans he'd be going with, and they got the reporter outfitted with camouflage uniform, a pistol belt, and canteens. He carried no weapons, but was loaded down with camera equipment.

The operation was to the west, always a hot area, and they got into heavy contact with the enemy about 0800 hours. Our troops took a couple of casualties, but managed to kill several VC and take a couple of prisoners. By early afternoon the patrol was back in camp, happy and flushed with their victory.

Bill pulled me off to the side the first chance he got. "That goddamned reporter is weird," he said. Then Bill told me a few details about what had gone on during the operation.

"He didn't want to stay with us in the command group, but kept trying to roam up and down the column. He's taking fucking pictures all the time, *click-click*. All of a sudden the point element runs into a Cong booby trap. *Wham!* We hear we got a wounded striker, then the shooting starts. We all run up to where the action is going on, and the reporter is right there with us, cameras bouncing and flopping around. Shit's flying everywhere, and the reporter's steadily taking pictures."

Bill paused for a second and lowered his voice. "We kill a couple of the Cong, and the strikers drag their bodies over to the canal bank so we can search 'em. The reporter asks us to cut their fucking heads off and stand there holding them like headhunters. He said it would make a real good photo!"

"So, did you do it?" I asked.

"Fuck no!" Bill laughed. "Think we're crazy? Pitzer gave him this lecture about how that was against the rules of war and how we don't do shit like that. We start to move up the canal a little ways, and luckily the reporter is back behind us with the tail squad. We run right into some of our boys interrogating one of the prisoners. They got the poor bastard spread-eagled on his back, and they're giving him the ol' water torture. That goofy squad leader from Second Platoon has a bamboo tube stuffed in the VC's mouth, wet rags around his nose and mouth, and another striker is pouring about five gallons of that nasty fucking canal water down his throat!"

I laughed. "That would have made a good picture for his magazine."

"Yeah, right," Bill said. "We ran over and got that little scene broken up just in time. When the reporter came around the bend, Pitzer was treating the prisoner, and everything looked okay."

The reporter stayed with us for a little over a week, and we all got to like him. We talked freely with him about the situation around Tan Phu and about our feelings toward the war. In '63 there had been little media coverage of the war in Vietnam, people at home didn't know anything about it, and we were anxious that they should get an idea of the true situation. We certainly weren't ashamed of anything, and in fact were proud of the job we were doing.

Within weeks of his departure his news article on Tan Phu hit the stands, and this was followed immediately by shit hitting the fan. We began getting our asses chewed out by higher headquarters on the radio before we had even received a copy of the article. When we did get hold of it, we saw what everyone was mad about.

His article, which appeared in one of the major photo-news magazines of the day, was the prototype for the many twisted, biased, antiwar pieces that were to follow in the coming years. It wasn't that he actually lied about anything, but the spin he put on things definitely was very unflattering.

There was very little in the article about the successful combat patrol we'd taken him on or about the medical patrols. The line the article took was the one that would become very popular on college campuses in upcoming years: the peace-loving Vietnamese would be just fine if the nasty, warmongering Americans would only go home. I remember one photo in particular. It was a picture he'd snapped of one of the village kids begging for candy. She was standing on the other side of a strand of concertina barbed wire, hand outstretched, looking beseechingly and pitifully at the camera. It looked like we had her locked up in a fucking concentration camp!

Our team took a lot of flak over that news article. Everyone in our higher chain of command was under the impression that we'd told the reporter all the crap he'd written, which was definitely not the case, of course. Conveniently forgotten was the fact that they had sent the bastard to us in the first place. What really pissed us off was not so much what the reporter had written, but that he'd betrayed our trust and friendship. His article was a real stab in the back.

Navarro and Pitzer were getting ready to make a trip into Saigon for supplies, and said if they ran into the reporter in town, they planned to whip his ass. Dan said later that he'd spent a good part of one day looking for the newsman and spreading the word around town what would happen if we found him.

"You should have seen the eyes of those reporters and rear-echelon pukes," Dan told us later. "I went storming into that fancy bar they all hang out at on the top floor of the Caravelle and told everyone there I was looking for that asshole so I could kick his butt. It surprised the hell out of 'em."

The next two people we sent to town also looked for the reporter, but they found out that he'd returned to the States. I never saw him or noticed his byline again during the course of the war, but I'm sure he was a huge success somewhere. Maybe he went to work for *Ramparts*. As things turned out, this wasn't our last visit from the media at Tan Phu, but our next encounter with the gentlemen of the press was to be much more pleasant.

Chapter 14

Several times during this narrative I've mentioned the interrogation of prisoners. I've hinted that occasionally these interrogations got a little rough, and I'm afraid this is certainly the case. That guy who said "war is hell" wasn't just whistling Dixie, and it gets to be even more hellish if you're unfortunate enough to be on the losing side.

Before I start going into the gory details of this subject, I want to say right up front that although all of us on the American team were witness to a lot of brutality, none of us was directly involved in it. All moral considerations aside, torturing a prisoner is not a good way to get any kind of useful information. The poor victim will say anything he thinks his tormentors want to hear just to end the ordeal.

By the start of the Vietnam War, plain old physical torture was old-fashioned and had been replaced by newer, more effective psychological techniques and the use of drugs. In our official role of "military advisers," we passed on this information to our LLDB counterparts. This was one area where our advice had very little effect, however, because like the graft and corruption, harsh treatment of prisoners was simply a fact of life in the Vietnamese military.

128

Prisoners were usually picked up during combat operations, although occasionally our men would catch a suspected VC agent skulking around the AO. The prisoners were held at camp for a few days while Pee Hole and his crew interrogated them, attempting to get any information that directly related to the situation around our area of operations. If the prisoner appeared to be a high-ranking VC or have extensive knowledge, he would be sent back up to higher levels of command for further questioning and possible imprisonment out at Con Son Island. If the prisoner wanted to defect, he was also shipped up the chain of command. We had a lot of latitude down at the A-team level, however, regarding what we did with prisoners.

During their internment at Tan Phu, the POWs were held in barbed-wire cages. These cages were about six feet square, and only high enough for a person to sit up in. The cages were out in an open area with no shade, and although the prisoners were furnished with food and water, I'm sure life in the cage must have been miserable.

After the first few weeks at Tan Phu, our team realized that we were pretty much cut out of the intelligence-collecting process and came to ignore what was going on.

"Noticed they got a couple of new ones in the cages," someone might mention at the breakfast table.

"Yeah? Any of 'em girls?" would come the disinterested answer.

If I got bored, I'd occasionally wander over and take a look at the captives. Usually they would stare back at me from where they crouched on the ground with blank, expressionless faces. Now and then we'd have a hardcore VC, and he would let me see the hatred in his eyes. I felt no pity or hatred for any of them, only curiosity.

The LLDB intel sergeant, Pee Hole, was in charge of

the interrogations, but he did very little of the dirty work himself. He had three or four little thugs he'd recruited from the strike force who took care of it. I've never understood why someone would want to be a professional torturer. The crew that did it at Tan Phu didn't seem to get any particular sadistic pleasure out of it, but went about their job in a very unemotional, businesslike manner. Somehow, this made it even worse.

The main interrogation room was over in the LLDB quarters, next to Phong's office. Any quiet, secluded spot would do, though, and you were liable to stumble on an interrogation in progress anywhere around camp. I tried to watch a couple of sessions but found I just didn't have the stomach for it. Too softhearted, I guess.

Most of the techniques used have been around for centuries. The first stage in an interrogation was to make the victim strip completely naked, then sit him on the floor while the interrogators stood or sat in chairs around him. This, naturally, put the prisoner at a big psychological disadvantage. The questioning would start in a casual manner, and if no answer, or the wrong answer, was given, the prisoner would receive a few slaps or punches—just enough violence to show that the interrogators meant business.

If the prisoner wasn't a committed VC, he would usually crack at this point in the process and spill his guts. The trick was to know whether he was telling the truth or not. Maybe he was a VC agent, a "plant" sent in with the mission of spreading some false information. Intelligence work is tricky business. This was also the point at which many prisoners said they wished to defect and join our side. Did they mean it, or were they trying to infiltrate our strike force?

If it appeared that this initial questioning would not produce any results, the POW was sent back to the cage for a while to "think things over." This was another psychological ploy intended to soften the prisoner up as he worried about what would happen to him next.

The next session would be worse than the first, and usually involved more sophisticated torture. The "water torture" that I mentioned in the previous chapter was one popular method. To perform this procedure, some sort of tube is jammed in the victim's mouth, wet rags are held over his nose, and water is poured down his throat. The victim tries to swallow it, but there's too much water, and he starts to drown, which is, of course, quite terrifying. Between each drowning, the prisoner is questioned again, knowing what awaits him if he does not answer the question.

Another technique was the same one we used on each other when we were kids. We used to call it "giving someone a pinky." To apply this technique, the torture squad would either hold or tie the victim down, then gently but methodically begin striking the same area on his body over and over again. The accumulated strikes, although each lightly applied, eventually irritate the nerve endings, causing ever-increasing pain. The beating was usually applied to the victim's forehead, stomach, or the bottoms of his feet.

One day I happened to walk past the LLDB quarters and heard a groan and cry of pain. I glanced in and saw that a man was hanging several feet off the ground by a rope. I looked closer and saw that he was the victim of a torture technique I'd once seen in a book about the Spanish Inquisition.

The victim of this technique first has his hands tied

behind his back, then a rope is run from his wrists up over a cross beam in the ceiling. As questioning begins, tension on the rope is increased, pulling the arms painfully upward behind the victim's back. Eventually the poor bastard is suspended in the air. If more pain is still desired, the rope is allowed to slip a foot or two, then suddenly jerked to a stop. This usually dislocates the prisoner's shoulders. If still more agony is required, one of the torturers can hang from the prisoner's legs.

Electric shock was the most popular method of torture used at Tan Phu. I suppose that the French introduced the Vietnamese to this high-tech means of inflicting misery, and by the early sixties it had been eagerly adopted by both North and South Vietnam. It had the benefits of being easy for the torturer to apply and of leaving no marks on the victim's body. There was usually a battery or, more likely, a field telephone around to use as an electrical supply, so it was a handy method too.

Usually the prisoner would be forced to hold one electrode in his mouth. The other lead was often wrapped around the man's penis. Getting shocked with the low current generated by the field phone was more terrifying than actually harmful, but I know of one occasion where a tough old VC was hooked up to a car battery. One of the electrodes was tied to the little toe of his right foot, which eventually turned black and probably had to be amputated.

That's about the extent of the torture methods I saw used around Tan Phu or any other place I was at during the Vietnam War. No one was flayed alive, slowly roasted over hot coals, or any of that business, and although the use of any form of torture can never be condoned, the methods Pee Hole used were no worse than what still goes on in many jails all over the U.S.

One interrogation I watched moved me more than any of the others, and it involved no torture at all. We had captured a wounded VC and were attempting to treat him in our dispensary. It was a serious head wound—a large piece of his skull had been blown away, and his brain was swelling and pushing out of the hole. There obviously wasn't much that could be done for him, and he was delirious. Pee Hole and a couple of his helpers were there trying to question him before he died. The prisoner thought one of the nurses was his wife, and that one of Pee Hole's goons was his brother. They were both playing these roles and trying to pump him for information.

The interpreter whispered in my ear, translating the conversation, which went something like this:

"Dear, I love you," the wounded VC said, "look out for the kids when I'm gone."

"Yes," the nurse replied, "I love you too. Where are the weapons and ammunition hidden?"

"Is that you, brother?" the VC said. "Please tell Mom and Dad good-bye for me."

"Yes, it's me," the goon answered, grinning. "I'll take care of them. Who is your battalion commander?"

He died, finally, without ever giving us any information, and his body, along with a couple of others, was put on display in the village.

One day, several weeks after we'd first arrived at Tan Phu, Phong and Pee Hole immediately recognized a middle-aged VC who was brought into camp. The prisoner had been captured, questioned, and sent up to higher headquarters several months previously. Phong was furious because he was a notorious VC, but had for some reason been released by higher authority. We didn't know if he'd bought or talked his way out. Anyway, he'd come right back into the AO and continued his activity, only to be recaptured.

A day or two later Phong came into our operations center and told us that after interrogation, the prisoner had agreed to show where some weapons were hidden up around the intersection of the main canal and Canal Seven.

"I send VC and one squad in boat to Canal Seven," Phong told us. "VC no show us weapons, then he try escape." He shrugged his shoulders. "Too bad for him, we must shoot, and he die."

That evening, this was reported to our higher headquarters in our daily sitrep. "One VC POW KIA while attempting to escape." Nothing was said about this by anyone. I mean, what were we supposed to do, call the camp commander a liar? We'd already seen what happened to Captain Leites.

As I said, we weren't keeping real close track of the prisoners who came and went around camp. A few weeks after this incident, Rowe happened to ask Phong about another man who was in the cage for a while and had then disappeared.

"Oh, we talk to him on the phone," Phong answered with a thin smile. "He important VC. We take Canal Seven . . ." Phong made a throat-cutting motion.

Pretty soon the phrase "taking a prisoner to Canal Seven" became sort of a grim joke on our team. There was a high turnover of prisoners around camp, and very few of them were sent up the chain of command. Of course, we never really knew if these people were really being killed or if some of them were simply being released. You might say we developed our own "don't ask, don't tell" policy.

Chapter 15

Only a few weeks after Hardy was evacuated, Jim Browning came on board to fill the intel slot. Jim was a sergeant first class then, but he'd once been a major. During the big reduction in force after the Korean War, Jim had been forced to give up his commission and return to enlisted grade. He didn't seem bitter about it, and said that if things heated up enough in Vietnam, he would probably regain his commission.

Cross was fully healed and had recently returned from a patrol, so I wasn't surprised when I got the word to prepare for the next one. This was to be a simple sweep, the kind of operation that later became known as a "search and destroy" mission. Browning and Pitzer were the other Americans going.

On this operation, I decided not to carry the PRC-10 myself, but to give that chore to one of the strikers. The LLDB radio operator, Dih Dah, had a couple of personal flunkies, and he offered to loan me one just for this duty. I'd already discovered that when on patrol, each American was expected to be a combat leader, and doing this while lugging around a radio was difficult.

I was still undecided about what kind of weapon to carry. Although many guys on the team still saw nothing wrong with the carbine, I'd lost all faith in it on my first operation. Captain Arsenault liked the M-3 "grease gun" for some reason and always carried that. The M-3 was small and didn't get in the way, but it was heavy, the .45 ammo was heavy, and because it fired from the open bolt position, there was no safe way to carry it that still allowed for immediate firing. Arsenault was a big, husky ex–football player, though, and the weight of the weapon didn't bother him.

Our team had recently received a brand-new type of weapon for field testing. It was called an M-79 grenade launcher, and the one we had at Tan Phu was probably the first M-79 ever used in actual combat. Everyone on the team fell immediately in love with this little weapon, and Pitzer began to carry it every time he went on patrol.

Lieutenant Rowe had gone back to the old M-1 Garand. The Garand was the weapon we'd all learned to use in basic training. It had been the Army's primary individual weapon until a couple of years before, when the M-14 was phased in, so it was the rifle we felt most comfortable with. We were all aware of its shortcomings, however, such as an eight-round magazine capacity. The damned Garand was also heavy, especially after one had carried the light, handy M-2A1 carbine a few times.

Since I'd relieved myself of the heavy radio, I decided to follow Rowe's lead and on this operation carry a Garand. The ammo for the M-1 came in preloaded, eight-round clips that were issued in cloth bandoliers, and as I stripped the magazine pouches off my web gear, I gave some thought to the grenade situation. I was constantly experimenting with ways to carry equipment and munitions in Vietnam, but I never fully solved the problem of hand grenades.

If you hung the grenades on the front of the harness somewhere, they got in the way when you were flat on your stomach, a position that a combat infantryman becomes quite used to. There really wasn't room to put them on your pistol belt, although the new magazine pouches we were issued for the M-14 had a place to attach them. On this patrol I tried a new approach. While digging around the supply room, I'd discovered an empty claymore bag. I put two smoke and two frags in the bag, then hung it on my right side. I slung the M-1 bandoliers on my left. My pistol belt still held my .45, knife, compass, first-aid pouch, and two canteens.

The operation pulled out of camp before first light, as usual, and we moved in a generally northwesterly direction. We had only a reinforced platoon, and although we were following secondary canals and trails, at first we made good time. Because we'd been on a winning streak for the last couple of months, the troops were in good spirits and confident. I felt a tug on my sleeve soon after we cleared the village and saw a flash of gold teeth. It was my pal, the platoon leader.

I was immediately glad I'd decided to carry neither the carbine nor the radio, because on the very first canal crossing I fell in, the water going completely over my head for a moment before I managed to kick off the muddy bottom and make my way to shore. What a way to start the day, I thought to myself.

The patrol made little sound as we pushed farther and farther toward the U Minh forest. I was proud to see how much our troops had improved even in the few short weeks since I'd last been out with them. Now when we stopped, they automatically faded into the shadows alongside the trail and took up defensive positions. There was no talk, none of them tried to light a cigarette, and their equipment didn't rattle. I hoped their marksmanship had improved a little bit too.

The plan of this patrol was simply to penetrate as deeply as we could to the northwest without being detected. When the sun came up, we would begin our sweep to the south, and then back east toward the camp. Once we'd moved a kilometer or two away from Tan Phu, we began to bypass any signs of habitation we came to. This involved leaving the dry trail and sloshing through the paddies, crossing small streams and fording several shallow canals without the benefit of even the rickety pole bridges. I was soaked already anyway, so it didn't matter to me.

Pushing through the thick vegetation that grew along all the trails and waterways was spooky, even though it was safer to do this than follow the obvious routes. I'd discovered that traveling through high elephant grass was particularly claustrophobic and something I hated to do. There was much of this in the area we traveled that night. Our speed of march slowed way down as our point element carefully cleared one danger area after the other and attempted to spot any trip wires or other booby traps.

I could feel the tension in our troops grow as we neared the dreaded U Minh. When we got into VC territory, we switched roles with the enemy, becoming dependent on the guerrilla tactics of surprise and speed in order to hit them and move out again before they could react. All of us who had been at Tan Phu for a while knew it would be unwise to allow an operation to get bogged down, or pinned down, in action near the enemy's base of support.

On this operation we were lucky, and by the time the

first streaks of light appeared behind us, we had progressed several kilometers without tripping a booby trap
or running into an early-warning trail watcher or ambush.
We moved to the bank of the nearest large canal to get
out of sight among the palm trees, then rested and
checked our equipment. I screwed in the long whip and
attempted a commo check with camp but got no
response.

Oh, fuck! I thought, feeling my stomach begin to knot
up. I glanced over toward the LLDB command group,
which consisted of Lieutenant Tinh and Sergeant Canh,
and saw that they were also on their PRC-10, jabbering
away with no obvious difficulty. I pulled one of the two
spare batteries from the backpack of the striker who
carried the radio, ripped off the plastic cover, and
plugged it in.

"Got you loud and clear," came Sidney's immediate
response.

I breathed a sigh of relief and sent him a short message
with our exact coordinates. I knew that back at camp,
Lowe and Ponce would be adjusting the mortar to give us
covering fire if we needed it.

Browning had a short conference with Tinh and Canh,
then came over to Dan and me, where we sat near the
radio. He spread out his map.

"We're going to follow this little stream that runs
south down to the next canal," he said, tracing the route
for us on the map. "It will probably be rough going
because of all the growth, but we'll have concealment.
There are several clusters of houses, here and here," he
said, again pointing to the map, "where Canh and Tinh
say we might find some Cong. If we can get down there

without being compromised, we might be able to surprise them."

Dan and I both agreed that it sounded like a good plan. We would be between the VC and the U Minh and coming from the direction opposite where they would usually expect us. I made one more radio contact to camp, told them we were moving out to our south, then took down the long whip and gave the handset back to the radio bearer.

Remembering my experience on the last operation, I opened the bolt of the Garand, popped out the clip of ammo, and wiped everything clean. The M-1 was a rugged, dependable weapon that would continue to operate under the worst possible conditions, but I'd learned my lesson the hard way about preventive mainte-nance. Dan groaned as he shouldered the heavy aid bag again, then gave the M-79 a quick check. Like most Spe-cial Forces medics, Dan was always as anxious to kill people as he was to heal them.

The route down the streambed was only about two hundred meters long, but it was a tough trip. As soon as we left the bank of the canal and began moving south toward the objective, we were in some very thick stuff. There was no trail at all, as the local villagers used the stream only for boat travel. On the banks grew a profu-sion of elephant grass, reeds, bamboo, vines, and man-grove. The sun was well up in the sky and it was very hot already. Not a breath of breeze made it through the mass of growth, and we were covered by swarms of mosqui-toes and gnats.

We moved in single file; the point element was respon-sible for finding the easiest way through the mess. Occa-sionally we would drop down into the stream itself and slowly slosh through the muddy, waist-deep water. Because this was not a frequently used route of travel, there wasn't much threat of hitting an ambush. Still, it was pretty damned nerve-racking to be down in the stream with the overgrown banks towering above and knowing that if you *did* get ambushed, you would be dead meat.

It took about an hour to travel that two hundred meters, and when we were finally near the objective, the patrol came to a sudden halt. We'd bunched up during the movement, and now we crouched in the dead silence broken only by the buzz of the mosquitoes. Several minutes ticked by as we waited, and each moment we sat there, the situation became more dangerous. I was with Dan, Browning, and Canh about a third of the way along the file from the point.

"Shit," Sergeant Browning whispered, "let's go up and see what the hell's going on."

At the front of the column we found the point man and the squad leader. After a short, whispered conversation in Vietnamese, Sergeant Canh told us the situation.

"He find trip wire for *dap loi*," Canh said. "Think VC very near now."

With the point man in the lead, we crawled through the high grass until we unexpectedly came to a well-used trail. The point man showed us the practically invisible piece of plastic fish line that stretched across it at about knee level.

Canh was irritated that something so minor was the cause of the holdup, and he disgustedly reached up with a knife to cut the trip wire. I was crouched about three feet from where one end of the line disappeared into the foliage, and as Canh prepared to cut the line, a sudden rush of thoughts passed through my mind. What was at the end of the trip wire? Was it merely one of the usual *dap loi*, or maybe a goddamned grenade or even something bigger? A booby trap can be rigged to go off when the line is either pulled or *cut*! Oh shit, I thought, and closed my eyes.

Luckily, nothing exploded, and when I got up enough nerve to look again, the line was cut and Canh was removing the small *dap loi* from where it was attached to a post.

The patrol pushed on, and within minutes we reached the canal bank. Although the area seemed deserted, there were several small boats moored at the edge of the canal. We commandeered these, sending one squad across to the opposite side. There was absolutely no talking now except in short whispers, and there was a palpable feeling of tension and expectancy in the air. You could damn near smell the VC lurking somewhere in the area.

Well spread out now, and moving slowly along the large, well-used trails on either side of the canal, we began our sweep back toward camp. After progressing only four or five hundred meters, we came to the first group of huts.

I had only a glimpse of the peaceful village scene playing itself out before me. Then we were spotted. Someone yelled in Vietnamese, and two young men in black shirts appeared suddenly from somewhere, running for cover. Hell, I thought, this is just like hunting birds. There were shouts from our men, a few bursts of fire, and a group of strikers led by the BAR man we called "Crazy" ran around the back of the buildings trying to cut off the fleeing VC.

Crazy wasn't so much nuts as he was simply dumb. In

a way, he made the perfect infantryman, being too stupid to know he'd been screwed getting stuck carrying a BAR and, more important, too dumb to be afraid of anything. There were more shouts and shooting from the direction of the chase, a short pause, then a long burst from Crazy's BAR.

The rest of us began a search of the small village, ordering the terrified old men, women, and kids out of the bunkers they had fled to at the first shots. They stood around in several small groups, silently watching as we dug around in their meager possessions. They remained impassive as Crazy and his bunch gleefully dragged the riddled body of one of the VC around the corner of a hut and dumped him on the packed earth at the doorstep.

We needed to search the body, but no one wanted to do it because Crazy had evidently emptied the entire magazine from his BAR into the bastard. Sergeant Canh finally had to order one of the strikers to perform the disagreeable chore. As usual, there was nothing of much interest on the dead man. He was wearing a pistol belt with one old American grenade on it; otherwise he wasn't even armed.

There was more than the usual amount of communist propaganda and paraphernalia in these huts, and the civilians were obviously not very happy to see us. Canh and Tinh attempted to talk with them, but the villagers were tight-lipped and would say very little. The two VC we'd flushed were apparently sons of someone in the village and had come home from their sanctuary in the U Minh for a little visit.

As we got reorganized and prepared to continue our sweep down the canal bank, I remembered the punch line from an old Lenny Bruce joke.

"Well," I chuckled to myself, "other than that, how did you enjoy your son's furlough, comrade?"

The shooting had, of course, given away our presence in the area, along with any further chance of surprising the enemy. We were about five kilometers from camp and in the sticky position of trying to get home without being shot to pieces ourselves by the alerted enemy. The urge was to simply return by the quickest, safest route, but we couldn't give the appearance of running away, either to our troops, to the VC, or to the local villagers in the area.

Leaving the dead VC where he lay for his family and friends to worry about, we started for camp. The chance of ambush or other enemy contact was much greater now, yet we still had to move swiftly. At the next group of houses, we stopped long enough for merely a cursory check of the area, then pushed on. We'd gone less than another hundred meters when we came under fire.

It was only harassing sniper fire, but it made us stop and duck for cover. The shooting was coming from the banks of another canal, which ran parallel to ours about three hundred meters to our north. A flat, open expanse of rice paddy stretched between our position and theirs. In the enemy tree line, I thought I could make out a little movement, maybe a spot of black uniform. I was glad I'd decided to carry the M-1, because this was a perfect range for the .30-06.

I was kneeling behind a palm tree and took up a good solid firing position, steadying the weapon against the tree. The rifle was sighted in for two hundred meters, so I held a little over the target and squeezed off a round.

I'd been a shooter since I was six years old and had qualified as an expert rifleman. With the experience that comes from firing thousands of rounds, I knew this shot was in there. Looking over the Garand's sights, I saw that the spot of black had disappeared and could discern no further movement.

Gotcha, didn't I, you son of a bitch! I thought as a wave of exaltation swept over me. It never even occurred to me to feel bad about killing him.

Dan came running up in a crouch and knelt on the other side of the tree. "Can you see where it's coming from?" he asked, flipping up the big leaf sight on his M-79.

Before I could answer, there was another burst of fire a little distance from where I'd first seen the enemy, and Dan spotted it. He adjusted the sights, took careful aim, and let one of the 40mm shells fly.

Several strikers nearby had been watching Dan with interest, having never seen the M-79 in action before. Because of the huge bore of the weapon, the anemic sound it made surprised them, and they began to snicker, apparently believing it had somehow malfunctioned. Moments later, when the shell detonated in the opposite tree line with an authoritative *crack*, their laughter stopped and their eyes grew large in wonder.

"Number-hucking-one!" they said, grinning with approval.

There was still scattered firing from the enemy position, but we got the troops up and moving anyway. I could tell by the worried look on the faces of several of our more experienced troops that they didn't like the situation we were in too much. I wanted to call camp and give them a quick briefing on what was going on, but to do that I'd have to stop long enough to put up the long whip, and there wasn't time.

So far, we had taken no friendly casualties, so we weren't slowed down by the necessity of carrying dead or wounded. Near the next canal intersection, however, there was another burst of fire, immediately followed by one of our strikers setting off a damned booby trap as he dove for cover. Now we did have someone wounded, and Dan hurried forward to see what he could do for the man.

We were forced to stop again and take up a temporary defensive position as Dan treated the wounded striker. Almost immediately we came under sniper fire, once again from the bank of the parallel canal. Apparently it was the same bunch following us, unintimidated and sure that we would not assault them across the open rice paddy . . . or maybe that's what they wanted.

"Better call camp and tell 'em what's going on," Browning said, squatting down beside where I sat with the Vietnamese radio bearer. I'd already started putting up the antenna.

"Shall we call in some 81s on the assholes?" I asked hopefully, the combination of fear and anger having sent my blood lust soaring.

"Not yet," Browning answered, "the LLDB are trying to contact the 155s at district. That ought to be enough to quiet down a few fucking snipers." He laughed, then hurried off to check on the wounded striker.

As occasional slugs cracked through the air, sending bark and leaves falling to the ground around me, I called camp and told Sidney the situation. While I was at it, I made a commo check with him using just the short whip antenna, and discovered we'd gotten close enough for it to work. This made me feel a lot better, because now we would have instant commo until we reached camp.

I'd just finished talking to Cross when I heard the

boom from the 155s at Thoi Binh. Two rounds whistled overhead and immediately burst in the rice paddy, short of their target. Two large geysers of water and rice paddy muck blew into the air. The enemy sniper fire came to a screeching halt, and I could imagine the startled VC hugging the muddy ground in fear. Tinh spoke excitedly into the handset of his PRC-10, and almost immediately there followed the sound of two more rounds on the way. These were airbursts and exploded just below treetop level directly over the enemy position. Our strikers cheered, laughing and jeering at the enemy.

Our wounded man was not critical and was still able to walk. Continuing on, once again full of confidence, our patrol headed for home. We received no more enemy fire, had no further contact, and in a few hours we passed our outpost line, smug and triumphant.

A few minutes later, wet boots off, equipment tossed in one corner, Browning, Pitzer, and I sat at the table in the Titis Tavern. We sipped large glasses of iced beer, laughing as we told the others how Crazy had shot the young VC twenty times, and how the 155s had blasted the snipers. It felt great to still be alive and uninjured ourselves, and as all the tension of the day washed away, it seemed like life couldn't be much better.

Chapter 16

Our strike force at Tan Phu had always been integrated with a few Cambodians. They made good, tough troops, and being in the minority, always seemed to try harder. In early October a group of four new Cambodians arrived and offered their services. They were hired, put to work on the strike force, and immediately showed signs of prior leadership experience.

Several weeks later they made secret contact with members of the American team, saying that they represented a group of Cambodians known as the Khmer Serei, whose headquarters were in Saigon. They were violently anticommunist, they told us, wanted to fight, and could bring others of their group down to join us if we gave the word.

We'd received intelligence briefings on the Khmer Serei on our arrival in-country and knew a little about them already. Their long-range objective was the overthrow of Prince Sihanouk in Cambodia. Other Special Forces units had previously worked with this group and reported good results, so we were more than willing to accept their offer. They told us they could furnish us a one-hundred-man company, complete with its own built-in chain of command.

There were two immediate problems. First of all, by making contact directly with our American team and bypassing the LLDB, they had gravely insulted Phong and his bunch. The Vietnamese already disliked all Cambodians simply on principle, so this really got things off on the wrong foot. Since the Americans were paying the troops' wages, there wasn't much Phong could say about this deal, but it didn't go over too big with him. He reminded us that there was also another group of Cambodians operating in Vietnam known as the Khmer Kampuchea Krom (KKK), whose goal was to restore to Cambodia several provinces of Vietnam.

The reputation of the KKK group was definitely unsavory. They were considered to be little more than bandits and had already been involved in at least one attempted revolt at another CIDG camp. They certainly weren't loyal to the South Vietnamese government, and they occasionally fought on the side of the VC when it seemed to suit their needs. Phong said that he didn't know any more about the workings of these various Cambodian groups than we did and that bringing in a complete company of them could be very dangerous. We finally decided to go ahead and bring the Cambodians into camp anyway, but not arm them at first, allowing us some time to check out their loyalty.

The Cambodians began arriving in small groups immediately after we gave the contact element the word, and by the final weeks of October we had added another hundred men to our strike force, bringing us up to four full companies. We gave the new Cambodians uniforms, but as planned did not issue them weapons yet. We put them to work pulling construction details and other such jobs around camp, and kept an eye on them.

We were authorized and prepared to recruit, train, and equip a strike force of up to battalion size, or about five hundred men, and we were quickly approaching this number. Although the VC still controlled things at night and continued their probes and harassment of the camp, we had been pretty successful at expanding our operational area. The intelligence reports we got from all our sources repeatedly indicated that very large, heavily armed, main-line units of VC were still in the area, but although continuing to take many casualties ourselves, we felt that we were slowly beating them.

There was constant pressure from higher up the chain of command, however, for us to be even more aggressive in our operations. I still had the distinct impression that the higher-ups took all our reports of enemy strength with a grain of salt. Sitting over cocktails on the top floor of the Caravelle Hotel, looking out over the glimmering lights of Saigon, it was, of course, hard for them to understand the situation we faced at a place like Tan Phu. The American regular Army—MAAGots, we called them—were jealous of Special Forces and did not understand the concept of the CIDG program. They had just regained control of American Special Forces units in Vietnam from the CIA and were anxious to show the Agency, whom the Army generals thought of as prima donnas, how to fight a war.

By late October 1963 the whole future of the LLDB, and consequently of the CIDG program, was in question anyway. Nhu continued to use a large part of the Vietnamese Special Forces as his own private SS/Palace Guard. He had continued to use them in his attacks on the Buddhists too, and due to political pressure, the CIA stopped their payments to the LLDB. Nhu was told the payments would not resume until the unit was reassigned from his personal control to that of the Joint General Staff.

Toward the end of this month, a series of events took place that set up the coming disaster we would face at Tan Phu on October 29. To begin with, Major Phong told us one morning that he was suffering from a recurrent liver ailment and would have to return to Saigon for a few weeks. He departed on the next helicopter, and command of the camp was assumed by the inexperienced Lieutenant Tinh.

In a way, life around Tan Phu was easier without Phong's presence. Tinh was basically a nice guy and a weak leader, so the Americans pretty much began running things around camp the way we wanted to. It was smooth sailing, there was much less tension in camp, and even the rank-and-file CIDG troops could tell the difference. Morale at Tan Phu rose to its highest level yet.

The downside of not having Phong around camp was that his sources of good intelligence information also dried up. We still continued to receive reports, but these were definitely not as trustworthy as the ones we'd gotten from Phong's personal agents.

Lieutenant Rowe had been unable to take R&R yet, but now that Arsenault was there and had his feet on the ground, he went into Saigon for a few days. Sometime during this trip, Rowe met a captain named Versace, thus setting up the chain of events that would lead them both to tragedy. Versace, known as "Rocky" to his friends, was the MAAG intelligence adviser in Camau. Rocky was a West Point graduate and had just volunteered for a six-month extension after completing a one-year tour of duty.

Rowe and Versace immediately became friends, and on the way back to camp Lieutenant Rowe stopped off at Camau with Versace for a visit. Special Forces and MAAG had no direct contact at this time, and the two officers understood that it would be to both units' benefit if we could start communicating with each other. MAAG could use our intelligence information, which apparently never got to Versace through the official chain of command, and we could certainly use any additional fire support, especially air cover, that Versace could direct our way.

Camau was about twenty-six kilometers south of Tan Phu, and we had no direct radio communications with them. Captain Versace loaned us one of their TR-30 voice radios, and we worked out an under-the-table, bootleg net. This means of communications was only partially successful, as there was no one on full-time radio monitor at the MAAG end, but it gave us one more way to call for help if we needed it, and we were all thankful for that.

Rowe made another trip to Camau for further coordination of our efforts and apparently was quite successful. When he returned, he told us he'd invited Versace to come out and visit camp so he could get a firsthand look at the situation. Since Versace was apparently a personal friend of Rowe, there wasn't much objection from anyone on the team, although none of us had much use for anyone from MAAG, whom we all considered to be pampered, overpaid paper-pushers.

Lieutenant Rowe had been doing all of this work on his own initiative without bothering to check with our new detachment commander, Captain Arsenault. Although Arsenault didn't say anything directly, you could tell it didn't sit very well with him, and I'm sure he had a feeling that his command was being usurped in some vague manner. I'm also sure that Arsenault was aware of the fact that "Rocky" and Rowe were both West Point "ring-knockers."

In those closing days of October, our team was already beginning to look forward to going home. Our six-month tour was more than half finished, and the big question was whether we would get relieved a week or two early so we could be home by Christmas, or whether we would have to spend the holiday at Tan Phu. Half the men on the team had already been wounded, and those of us who hadn't were beginning to look at each other and secretly wonder which one of us would be next.

We had all lost a lot of weight since we'd been there, with the exception of Lieutenant Rowe, who actually managed to gain a few pounds. We joked and teased him about this, telling him that no one would believe he'd been in Vietnam if he returned fatter than when he left. Halloween was quickly approaching, and we also laughed about how at Tan Phu we already had our own nightly version of trick or treat, compliments of the VC.

Chapter 17

Captain Versace arrived unexpectedly early one afternoon. We had already wasted the entire morning conducting a dog-and-pony show for a touring MAAG colonel who had dropped in with his entourage of ass-kissers and flunkies, so we weren't overjoyed to hear again the sound of incoming choppers.

"Who is it this time," I asked Cross, "the fucking USO?"

There were two HU-1Bs, one of them armed. This was a good indication that the other chopper, a slick, contained another big shot. The choppers buzzed the camp unnecessarily to alert us of their intention to land, the downwash from their blades blowing thatch from our roofs.

"Grab a green smoke, Wade," Rowe told me, as disgusted as everyone else at this further interruption to our busy daily schedule. "We'll go out and meet them."

I grumbled a "yessir" and started looking for my beret. The only time we wore them at Tan Phu was when we had visitors.

We walked out the main gate to our landing pad, and I tossed the smoke to indicate to the pilots they were clear to come in. The lieutenant and I held our berets on our heads as the slick landed. The armed Huey continued to orbit overhead. A dark-haired captain, his clean, starched fatigues and baseball cap marking him as a REMF, hopped to the muddy ground, and the crew chief tossed out his bags behind him. The chopper rose in the air again and departed.

Suddenly smiling, Rowe walked over to the captain, saluted, then shook hands. "Hi, Rock," the lieutenant said, "welcome to the end of the world."

Rowe introduced me to Versace, who, so help me, had arrived carrying his own portable Thermofax machine. Then the two of them headed toward camp as I tailed along behind, carrying Versace's luggage. The striker at the front gate, hoping to score some points, snapped to attention and saluted them as they passed through. Me, he just grinned at.

I'll admit Tan Phu looked like a real slum. There were clothes hanging on the barbed wire to dry, nasty, yellowish water standing in the moat, and chickens pecking around on the ground. Our pet dog, Pluto, lay directly in the path leading to the team house, lazily licking his balls, and we had to walk around him. Sure, the place didn't present a very good first impression, but it was still our home.

Versace had been looking around with a slight sneer on his face ever since he got off the helicopter. As we entered the dirt-floored team house, the sneer deepened. Rowe introduced Versace to Arsenault and the other team members interested enough to come over to find out who'd arrived. There was an empty canvas cot in the operations room, and I dropped Versace's crap on it.

"Where should I plug this in at?" Versace asked, referring to his copier.

"You can put it over there next to the map table, sir," I told him. "I'll have to run a line in from the generator for it—the five-kilowatt is down for repairs right now and we're trying to make do with the one point five. Hope it will pull the current." I didn't bother trying to explain to him that we ran the generator for only a few hours every evening to power the radio while we sent the sitrep. Every time he wanted to operate his fucking copier, I'd have to go out and fire up the generator, wasting gasoline and putting more hours on the already worn-out machine.

We had about twenty bags of Portland cement stored in the operations center. It was there both to keep it dry and to prevent pilferage. Versace looked at it, then looked around at all of us. "Why don't you try to fix this dump up a little? You've got the damned cement."

Although he didn't say it, the tone of his voice indicated that he thought we were probably too lazy to do it and preferred to live in the mud like pigs. He was really getting off to a bad start.

Rowe answered, obviously embarrassed to have been the person responsible for bringing this ignorant desk jockey into our midst. "We'd like to, believe me, but cement can only be used for civil affairs projects in the village. If we ever do have any left over, we'll use it for defensive positions."

Versace accepted this explanation without further comment, and whether he knew, or cared, that he'd pissed off everyone didn't show in his face. I was already wondering how long we'd have to put up with this guy around camp.

Sergeant Lima handed a five-page sitrep to Cross. "I'd help you encrypt that," I said in a voice I hoped was loud enough to be overheard by our visitor, "but I've got a priority mission to run a fucking electrical outlet instead."

For the next couple of days, Rowe attempted to be the good host and friend and act as Versace's escort on the standard tours of the area we always took visitors on. I could tell that this was irritating Captain Arsenault. Arsenault figured that he, being a captain also, and the detachment commander, should be the one to do this. He began to tag along with the two of them, and eventually Rowe obligingly bowed out of the picture, glad to be able to return to his many other duties.

In the meantime, we'd gone through almost an entire fifty-five-gallon drum of gas while Versace copied reams of our old intel reports, after-action summaries, and so forth. Finally the bulb burned out on his machine, and luckily, he had no spare.

On the morning of October 28, Versace happened to mention at the breakfast table that he'd like to take a run down to Thoi Binh to visit the district chief. Because Versace was with MAAG, he was in an advisory and staff position with district. Arsenault jumped at the chance to get out of camp and hurried over to the LLDB to coordinate a boat patrol down the canal.

I was overjoyed at the prospect of having both captains out of camp and out of my hair for a few hours, and I'd just gotten started on some maintenance on the 1.5-KW generator when I was notified by a grinning Sergeant Cross to grab my shit, pick up a PRC-10, and get my ass down to the boat dock.

A boat patrol to Thoi Binh wasn't a big deal, and although a person was never safe anywhere around Tan Phu, I didn't see why Arsenault thought he needed an American radio operator. When I got to the dock on the canal where we moored the Fiberglas assault boats, I saw that VandeBerg was also going along.

A simple run down to district had been turned into a huge production, I presumed for the benefit of our MAAG visitor. Lieutenant Tinh was going, we were taking all four boats, and a couple of squads were already moving out on either side of the canal bank to sweep the area for possible ambushes. I loaded the PRC-10 in one of the front seats of the boat, made a quick commo check with Cross, then sat down next to it, my weapon pointing out.

When in the immediate vicinity of camp, and while on these boat operations, I'd begun carrying a Model 97 riot gun. There's always been a lot of discussion about the usefulness of shotguns in war, but the effectiveness of the weapon at ranges of up to thirty yards has never been in question.

I'd timed myself, and knew I could unload seven rounds from the pump-action riot gun in under four seconds. With each 00 buckshot round containing nine slugs, this made for a lot of lead flying downrange in a short period of time. One of the main drawbacks to the shotgun was that it was slow to reload. The main danger on boat operations was being ambushed, however, and I figured that by the time I'd need to reload, I'd either be out of the kill zone or already dead.

The trip down the canal was uneventful, as I expected it to be. Once there, Van went over to the little Vietnamese aid station to see if he could help with anything. All the big shots went over to the district chief's office for their powwow, leaving me with nothing to do but sit around wasting time I could have been spending much more profitably back at camp.

An hour passed, and about noon I got the word that the command group had been invited to have lunch with the district chief. No mention was made of Van and me, and I was just as glad not to be a part of it anyway. One of our Vietnamese boat operators saw I wasn't eating and brought me a bowl of noodle soup.

Another couple of hours passed, during which I ran out of cigarettes. I was watching the artillery unit cleaning their 155s when Arsenault, Versace, and Tinh came walking quickly out of district headquarters, excitedly talking among themselves. You could feel the excitement in the air as we hurriedly loaded the boats and prepared to make the return trip.

I got on the radio to camp and told them we were heading back. Van and I were in the second boat, and the officers followed in the third. "You got any idea what's going on?" I asked VandeBerg.

"Who knows?" he said. "Probably more grandstanding bullshit."

Later that evening, I went in the commo bunker where Sidney was just finishing up with the day's radio traffic. "Looks like I'm not going on the operation tomorrow after all," I told him. "We'll still need to get a PRC-10 ready, but one of the Vietnamese will carry it."

"Is Versace still going?" Cross asked me, leaning back in the chair and putting his bare feet up on the table in front of him.

"Looks like it," I answered. "He can't get his L-19, but he's going anyway." I put a fresh battery in one of the 10s and cleaned off the connection on the handset before attaching it. MAAG personnel were not allowed to go on combat operations unless there was an L-19 flying over- head. Of course, MAAG personnel were not supposed to accompany anything smaller than a battalion-size operation and weren't allowed to be involved with CIDG operations at all.

"He's just gotta get that ol' CIB, huh?" Cross said with a chuckle.

"I'm glad I'm not going," I said, flipping the radio on and listening to the zero beat. "I've got a real bad feeling about this abortion. The whole damned thing is in response to some bullshit intelligence from district, and it was thrown together too fast. This Le Coeur place they're going to is way the hell over on the edge of the U Minh."

"Well," Sidney said, "by this time tomorrow they'll all be back sitting around telling war stories, and someone will be busily filling out the paperwork for Versace's CIB." Cross swung his feet to the ground. He flipped on the PRC-10 we used for the base station in the commo bunker. "Let's see if that fucking piece of junk works," he said, referring to the radio I was preparing for the operation.

Chapter 18

As I watched the reaction force cautiously slogging through the knee-deep water of the rice paddy toward camp, the first thing I noticed was that they were all armed with 9mm submachine guns. Unlike our own troops, they also all wore steel helmets, and many of them even had on flak vests. Once the reaction force completed their movement through the front gate of camp, Bill and I brought up the rear with our LZ security. I had fully expected the VC to mortar the piss out of us while we were in the wide-open rice paddy, but not a round fell. I was feeling a little better about our situation all the time, although things were still in doubt. The big question now was, what next?

It was dark already. We'd never attempted night offensive operations at Tan Phu, but then, we'd never had Americans missing in action before either. This Vietnamese SF company looked pretty good, especially compared to our ragtag bunch of strikers, but how good would they be at night? We knew there was a whole shitload of VC out there, and they would be waiting for us. I was glad I didn't have to be involved in making the decision of what to do next.

After a discussion between Arsenault, our LLDB, and

the reaction force company commander, it was decided that it would be best to put the reaction force on the walls, try to hold what we had left, and go out at first light to sweep the battle area. I believe this was the only real option we had and breathed a sigh of relief that we wouldn't be out stumbling around in the dark all night being decimated.

Frankly, we'd been thoroughly trounced that day. After several months of continuous victory, our once confident strike force was in shambles. Many of the survivors of the operation had arrived back at camp minus not only their weapons, which they had thrown down when they ran away, but also minus their complete uniforms. Most of our best troops, the brave ones who had held their ground and fought, were either missing, wounded, or dead. My pal, the gold-toothed platoon leader, had made it back to camp, but was missing his lower right arm.

Lieutenant Tinh had several wounds, but was still trying to carry on. Dih Dah, though only grazed on the arm by a bullet, had gone into seclusion. Canh was unwounded and doing a damned good job, but Pee Hole, our team's favorite LLDB member, was also missing in action. Although our ability to hold the camp itself had earlier been seriously in question, now that we had a hundred fresh reinforcements on the walls, I breathed a lot easier.

It was still a long, tense night. There were constant probes, mortar attacks, and sporadic firing until sunup. Ponce and Lowe kept the area lit up with illumination from the mortars. We would have liked to fire some HE interdiction, but because we still had many men missing out in the battle area, we dared not take the chance of hitting them. VandeBerg and his medics were swamped, of course, trying to save those they could. Van lost many patients that night.

Cross and I had our hands full with the radio, sending updates every fifteen minutes to the B-team. Captain Arsenault had finally been able to spend almost an hour with us in the commo bunker personally answering questions from the B-team commander about the situation.

Higher headquarters at MAAG had just found out that their G-2 officer from Camau was MIA, compliments of Tan Phu, and as if we didn't have enough problems, we were already beginning to feel the backlash this produced. We received an ominous message telling us to expect many visitors the next day.

As the sun was just coming up over the horizon, we heard the distinctive drone of an L-19 spotter plane overhead. Soon it was joined by four armed T-28s.

"This is your basic case of being a day late and a dollar short," I told Sidney.

"Sure, now that it's too fucking late, here comes the cavalry," Cross answered, his eyes mirroring the exhaustion I knew must show in my own.

The leader of the Cambodian company came into the Titis Tavern, where the American team, Tinh, Canh, and the reaction force commander all huddled around a map, making plans. He said his men were now fully armed, equipped, and anxious to be allowed to go on the upcoming operation. It was the only fresh, undamaged CIDG company we had left, and we agreed to allow the Cambodians to show us their stuff.

Besides the Cambodians, we scraped together another fifty able-bodied men from the remainder of our strike force, and by 0700 hours our troops were out the front gate and heading for the battlefield. Several of us on the team accompanied them, anxious to have the chance of helping our missing teammates but also dreading the possibility of finding their bodies.

I went with the reaction force company and was immediately aware of the fact that they seemed to know what they were doing. It was a great relief to simply move along with them without the added pressure of constantly trying to advise and train them at the same time. Their leaders knew their jobs, so I was also relieved of the leadership burden. Overhead the L-19 orbited and the T-28s buzzed around like angry wasps. I actually wasn't very concerned about making heavy enemy contact that day, figuring that the Cong had probably followed standard guerrilla tactics by retreating back to their safe area.

Hell, I thought to myself, this is the way to fight a war. If every operation we went on was like this, we'd really kick some butt. I daydreamed what it would be like if I was with a force of 250 American paratroops and decided we'd be invincible.

It wasn't difficult to find the scene of the previous day's battle. All we had to do was follow the trail of discarded clothing and equipment our routed troops had left behind as they ran for their lives. We came to the first group of thatch-roofed, mud-walled houses near where the action had taken place, and the platoon leader I was with barked a command.

The stern-faced reaction force members weren't as polite with the local civilians as our own troops were, and herded the cowering old men, women, and kids out of hiding with occasional punches, slaps, and butt strokes from their submachine guns. They'd recently had a lot of practice doing this sort of thing under Nhu's leadership.

The short interrogation of the terrified villagers was harsh and unpleasant.

"Have you seen any Americans, either dead or alive? Have you seen a Vietnamese wearing a camouflage uniform like mine?" Negative answers were rewarded with kicks and punches. This group of civilians knew nothing, and we pushed on.

We began finding occasional dead bodies, mostly our own strikers, but also one or two VC. As we got into the area where the heaviest fighting had taken place, the dead were in groups where they had made last stands before being overrun. It was grim business having to check each bloated, fly-covered corpse, rolling it onto its back to look at the contorted and sometimes mangled face, hoping each time it wouldn't be one of my friends.

Near one small village where we stopped for lunch we discovered a group of our dead in a line, sprawled with their faces in the mud. Some had their elbows tied behind their backs, two or three had already been wounded and wore battle dressings. All had been shot once in the back of the head, the ghastly exit wounds in their faces making identification that much harder. Several had been extensively mutilated, by what means I couldn't tell.

As I sat with my back against a palm tree, eating a can of C-ration peaches and talking with the interpreter, the reaction force commander brought one of the village women over to us.

"She say she see American alive," the tough little leader told me. He nudged her, and the old woman rattled off a couple of sentences in Vietnamese, speaking to the interpreter and me.

"She say she see VC have one American prisoner," the interpreter translated. "She say he have arms tied."

"Ask her how old he was, how tall," I said to the interpreter.

She listened to the questions, then answered, looking directly at me this time, defiance in her eyes.

"She say he young man, same size you—" He hesitated a moment. "She say he cry."

We searched the area until late in the afternoon, recovering our own dead and leaving the VC bodies where they lay. We continued interrogating any of the local villagers we could find and received many conflicting, inconclusive reports. From what the old woman had told us, it sounded like Rowe might have been captured, but we had other reports from people saying all three Americans had been seen dead or at least seriously wounded. We didn't find any American bodies, however, or any that we could identify as that of Pee Hole, so we had hopes that they were all POWs, or maybe even still out evading the enemy, trying to make their way back to Tan Phu.

Around 1600 hours we called it a day and returned to camp. We were weary and dejected and felt none of the elation that usually accompanied the end of an operation. There were two helicopters on our landing pad, and the visitors we'd been warned to expect were still at camp. The B-team commander was there along with some of his staff. There were also a couple of high-ranking officers from MAAG.

As I slumped in a chair in the Titis Tavern, sipping a glass of iced tea, I could hear loud, angry voices coming from the operations room next door. Although I had been warned to expect something like this, I was still a young, naive soldier and had not yet personally been involved with one of the inquisitions that must always follow a military disaster.

What was being played out was the game of "Who Gets Pinned with the Blame for this Mess?" The object of the game is to find the lowest-ranking individual who can logically be blamed, then dump on him. I soon found out that Cross and I were being seriously considered as prime scapegoat candidates.

Sidney came into the Tavern and sat down next to me. "Watch everything you say," he whispered in my ear. "The bastards are out to get us."

"What the hell do you mean?" I whispered back.

"Shit is rolling downhill," Cross said. "MAAG is blaming the B-team for not reacting fast enough. The B-team is blaming us, saying we never asked for help until it was too late."

"Oh, I get it," I said, starting to see the light and really getting pissed. "It was all commo's fault because we never sent any messages, right?"

"You got it," Cross said. "I think I already took care of things, though. I showed them our message log and file of in/out messages. There wasn't much they could say after that."

I silently thanked Captain Leites for his "advice" on how to keep commo records. Before the inquisition team left that afternoon, I was taken aside and interrogated about the previous day's action. All during the ordeal I was thinking that there were a few questions I'd like to ask them too, but the system didn't work that way, of course.

In the turmoil of the next few weeks the ill-fated operation of October 29 was soon forgotten. I don't know if anyone got blamed for it. In my own mind the one who should be blamed, or, depending on whose side you were on, credited, with the operation, was the VC commander who planned and executed it all. We had neatly been fed bait, drawn out into the battlefield of the enemy commander's choosing, then very expertly cut to pieces. I hope that the VC commander got the medal he deserved for a job well done.

After all the brass got in their helicopters and returned to their cushy quarters, clubs, cocktails, mistresses, and so forth, those of us at Tan Phu got ready to spend another night fighting for our lives. We were all sitting around the table in the Tavern, tired, downcast, and not talking much. Big John Lowe mentioned something that was probably nagging at all of us.

"Anyone happen to find Pitzer's M-79?" he asked, looking around the table. None of us had.

"Man, I hope the hell the VC didn't get it," Lima said, echoing what we all were thinking. "They could bring some real smoke on our asses."

We had become accustomed to listening for the distinctive sound that the VC mortars made as they left the tube, and this gave us some time to duck for cover before the rounds reached us. The M-79 made so little noise when it was fired, however, that if a determined VC should infiltrate within range and plunk one of the 40mm HE rounds into camp, we would have no time to react.

"How many rounds did he have with him?" someone asked.

"I think he was carrying ten," I said.

"Maybe he fired all, or most, of them," someone said hopefully.

"Maybe he managed to ditch the damned thing," someone else offered. "Dan was an experienced troop."

"Maybe he's still out there carrying it. Maybe he and Rowe will be at the front gate tomorrow morning yelling for breakfast," VandeBerg said.

"Yeah, and Versace will be with them hollering for me to fire up the generator so he can copy some more files!" I said, laughing.

None of us really believed any of this hopeful talk, though. I think that in our hearts we had written off the possibility of ever seeing them again.

Chapter 19

The next day, the last day of October, the reaction force again took to the field. This time they swept the perimeter of the battleground, questioning more villagers, looking for stray or wounded strikers, and hoping to catch a few VC. There was no contact with the enemy, although the intelligence gathered answered some of our questions about what had happened on the twenty-ninth. From what we could determine, our operation had been attacked by an enemy force larger than battalion size. We were starting to think in terms of a possible VC regiment.

This Vietnamese SF reaction-force company continued to impress me with their professionalism, and I hoped they were having a positive influence on our own strikers. As soon as they returned to camp in the evening, the reaction force performed maintenance on all their weapons and equipment, detail-stripping the weapons, even disassembling the submachine-gun magazines to clean out the silt. I really liked having them in camp and hoped they would stay with us for a while.

A few of our missing strikers continued to trickle into camp. Most of them were practically naked and were very ashamed of their cowardly conduct. I'm sure that many of the strikers whom we never heard of again refused to return simply due to this tremendous loss of face.

We began trying to count up our losses. So far we'd accounted for fifty or sixty dead, about the same number of wounded, and another twenty or thirty still MIA. Three Americans were MIA along with one LLDB. We'd lost enough weapons, ammunition, and equipment to supply a couple of VC companies.

Major Phong ended his stay in Saigon and also returned to camp on the last day of October. As things turned out, leaving the capital city probably saved his life. Phong was concerned about our major defeat and deftly retook command of the camp. He kept his face a typical "inscrutable Oriental" mask, but I'm sure he probably wanted to scream, "See, as soon as I'm gone you screw everything up!"

In the early-morning hours of November 1, all hell broke loose over at the LLDB headquarters. The reaction force, which was supposedly preparing to again depart on another sweep of the area, instead excitedly fell out and stood in formation while their company commander made a speech. Our counterparts, the LLDB team, all appeared wearing full battle gear, including their steel pots, something they'd never done before.

"What's going on?" Lima asked a grim-faced Canh as the little LLDB team sergeant went hurrying past.

"Is very bad," Canh told Lima. "I no have time tell you now—you find out pretty soon!"

None of us on the American team had any idea what the hell was going on. Over at the LLDB radio bunker, Dih Dah was frantically sending and receiving traffic, but when Cross attempted to make a commo check with our

B-team, he was given a terse "Stand by, out." I was starting to wonder if North Vietnam had launched a full-scale invasion.

Finally someone on the team got the idea to turn on our little battery-powered civilian radio. We kept it tuned to the Armed Forces Radio Station, which broadcast from Saigon. The initial reports were sketchy, as usual, but it appeared that there was a coup taking place in Saigon. Diem and his brother were in hiding somewhere. There was some fighting going on around the palace, and Americans were warned to stay indoors.

All that day we listened to developments on AFRS. We received a short message through channels finally, outlining the situation and telling us that Americans were not to get involved. The only resistance to the coup was being put up by the Vietnamese Special Forces defending the palace itself. They were evidently the only troops who'd remained loyal to Diem and seemed to be fighting to the death. It was their finest hour.

That evening, Phong and Canh came over to the Titis Tavern where the American team sat around the radio, listening to AFRS. Phong looked worn out and dejected.

"Very bad now for LLDB," he told us, looking around the table. We could do nothing but nod.

"Maybe LLDB must leave camp, go fight in jungle," he said.

This bombshell was greeted with a moment of stunned silence from the Americans, then Lima cleared his throat. "You mean join the VC?" he asked Phong.

"No VC," Phong answered with the trace of a smile. "VC fight, we fight, everyone fight."

"How will you survive?" someone on the team asked him. "What will you do for food, ammunition . . . ?"

Phong gave a derisive grunt. "No problem," he said. "VC can do; we can do. I was Viet Minh for many years."

"What about the strike force?" someone else asked.

"I take my team and the reaction force," Phong said. "If CIDG want go with us, okay, if not, stay here in camp with you." After a short silence, he added, "Maybe not happen. I wait one day, try to find out more information. Maybe everything okay tomorrow."

"Holy shit!" someone said as soon as Phong and Canh had departed. "It's not enough we have to fight the whole fucking Viet Cong army, now this!"

"I don't think the CIDG will go," I offered. Frankly, I didn't think they had the guts for the kind of thing Phong was suggesting, and the rest of the team agreed with me. I didn't believe that Phong wanted to do it either, but if pushed into a corner and given no choice, he might. The last we'd heard, the Palace Guard was still holding out. If Diem managed to escape and go into exile someplace, Phong could not very well surrender without losing tremendous face, especially after the example of bravery by the group defending the palace.

Evidently the coup leaders had taken Phong and our LLDB reaction force company into consideration, because late the next morning there were new developments. A small emissary of regular Vietnamese infantry arrived by boat unexpectedly and immediately went into conference with Phong. They were there only a short time, then left again.

"Now one battalion of rebel Vietnamese army surround camp," Phong told us. "They wait see if we fight for Diem or join them in coup."

Our situation at Tan Phu was getting wilder and more

confused all the time. We sat in the center of a bull's-eye surrounded by a group of hostile, regular Vietnamese infantry, who were in turn surrounded by a regiment of VC. To say the situation was highly volatile would be a huge understatement.

Night was approaching. We didn't want to fight the ARVN infantry unit, but if the VC hit us with a probe, we would have to fight back. If we started shooting, the ARVN unit might think we were attacking them and return fire. Also, if the VC hit the ARVN battalion, they might think it was us and begin shooting at camp.

"This is Vietnamese problem," Phong told our assembled American team. "If fighting starts, you go to bunkers, wait until over."

It was nice of Phong to let us off the hook this way, and what he said about it not being an American problem was surely the truth. But it didn't sit very well with the A-23 members.

"Major Phong," Arsenault said, "Tan Phu is our camp too, and if shooting starts, we aren't going to hide in the bunkers, no matter who is shooting at us. If we come under attack, we'll go to our battle positions as usual. If an actual ground assault is made against us, we will fire back to help defend the camp. If we are only taking some indirect fire, or if it looks like it's only a VC probe, we'll fire illumination from our 81 mortar, but no HE until we can positively identify the target."

Phong accepted this, glad of our support, and went back to his quarters.

"You know what really pisses me off about this?" I asked Cross. "We've been here for four months fighting swarms of VC and have never seen any support from this

ARVN battalion. When they finally do show up in our AO, it's to kick *our* ass!"

We spent that night on one hundred percent alert with every troop we had at their positions on the walls. There was some very minor action on the outpost line, and things got pretty tense for a couple of hours, but we had some real luck and the VC were not too aggressive that night. I'm sure the VC had no idea what a touchy situation we had around Tan Phu and were probably scared off by the presence of the infantry battalion camped outside our perimeter.

By the next morning, information from AFRS indicated that the coup was a success. Fighting around the palace had ended, and Diem and Nhu were dead, supposedly by suicide. The LLDB commander, Colonel Le Quang Tung, had also been bumped off.

The ARVN battalion sent another message to us telling Phong that the unit's commanding officer wanted to have a personal conference. Phong wasn't about to go out to the ARVN encampment, not only for fear of being captured, but because it would be a grave loss of face if it appeared that he was responding to a summons. The ARVN battalion commander wisely agreed to come to Tan Phu for the meeting, and about noon he arrived by boat with a few members of his staff.

No one on the American team was involved with this meeting, but several of us managed to peek into Phong's office to check things out. The meeting was very formal, yet with no signs of animosity between the two Vietnamese officers. Phong's flunkies served tea and a large meal of several courses while they discussed the problem. The battalion commander was in Phong's office for several hours, then he and his staff again departed.

"Is *fini*," Major Phong informed us. "I tell him I only want to fight VC, and battalion go back to Camau."

That was the second major crisis in a week, and all of us on the American team breathed a giant sigh of relief that it was over.

Chapter 20

A week later the reaction force was pulled out of Tan Phu. They returned to Saigon, where they were disbanded and reorganized under the new leadership. At Tan Phu we experienced a few days and nights of peace, which was quite unexpected by all of us. We'd assumed the VC would attempt to take immediate advantage of the disorganization within the Vietnamese leadership, but they failed to do so.

The short lull in enemy activity didn't last long, however. We were in the process of rebuilding our strike force, and consequently were forced to curtail many of our offensive operations. We weren't going as deeply into enemy-held territory as before, and we were not as aggressive. As soon as the VC figured this out, they pushed in to fill the void.

Around the immediate vicinity of Tan Phu, Diem had actually been very popular. As far as our situation at camp went, the coup had been a huge mistake. It was no longer as easy as it had been before the coup for us to recruit new strikers.

Of course, our major defeat on October 29 didn't do a lot to boost our recruiting efforts either. Prospective strike force members now saw that working at Tan Phu might not be the gravy train they were looking for. The district chief's small RF/PF group had sustained heavy casualties on the twenty-ninth too, and they were also recruiting like mad, giving us competition in luring prospective fighters.

Our biggest competitor for new recruits was, naturally, the VC. Unfortunately, the Cong tended to attract the tougher, more motivated young men in our area. Where we offered money, uniforms, and a snug bed, the VC offered nothing but hardship and an ideal.

Now that our First and Second companies at Tan Phu had been practically wiped out, the all-Cambodian Fourth Company took over as our best unit. These Cambodians had received military training someplace prior to coming down to us, and their leadership was sound. The biggest problem with them was that the LLDB and the rest of our Vietnamese strikers didn't like them, and the Cambodians themselves tended to exacerbate the problem by constantly brown-nosing the American team.

It didn't take Phong long to react to this state of affairs, and the Cambodians soon found themselves "under investigation" by the LLDB. All the Cambodians in leadership positions were placed under house arrest one morning, and an inquisition was launched. The supposed purpose of the investigation was to ensure that the unit was loyal to the Vietnamese government, but the real purpose was to break the leaders and make sure they understood who ran things around Camp Tan Phu.

As usual, there wasn't much our American team could do other than attempt to remain neutral and try to put in a few good words for the Cambodians, who had all been doing a hell of a fine job ever since the big battle.

Again things got pretty damn hairy around Tan Phu. Tensions were high as the Cambodian leaders were questioned individually, each one receiving variations of the third-degree techniques I described earlier. The Cambodian troops were all armed now, after all, and although outnumbered by the Vietnamese, an internal gun battle could have kicked off at any moment.

This situation lasted for the better part of a week before the Vietnamese decided to end it. We had a formation of the entire strike force during which the cowed Cambodian leaders swore allegiance to the Republic of Vietnam, to Camp Tan Phu, and, I supposed, to Major Phong. Then we all tried to get back to the job of fighting the VC.

A visitor from the B-team told us that we would soon be hosts to two more members of the news media. We were obviously not too happy to hear this, but we were assured that these two reporters weren't like the first guy and would give us a fair break.

A day or so later the two newsmen, who worked for *Look* magazine, came in by helicopter. Their names were Sam Castan and James Karales, and they told us they usually worked as a team. Castan was a writer and Karales took the pictures. Castan and Karales were good guys and immediately fit right in. We told them of our experience with the other newsman, and they agreed that we'd gotten the shaft.

It was fun listening to the stories the two reporters told about their many and varied assignments. Joan Baez was a very popular singer in the early sixties, and they had recently done an article on her. Jim and Sam kept us in stitches talking about their first meeting with Miss Baez, who at that time was still just a young, beatnik folk-singer, uninvolved with anti–Vietnam War protests.

The newsmen accompanied us on several combat operations, and they were quite courageous. During an operation they went on with Navarro and Martin, the patrol was in the middle of an open rice paddy when they were taken under fire by machine guns and mortars.

Karales continued to click pictures as the slugs and shrapnel flew and was right behind Navarro and Martin as they led the strikers in an impromptu assault on the enemy-held tree line. Karales got many good photos that day of some combat action for which Navarro was later awarded the Bronze Star.

The article they wrote, which appeared several months later, was honest and pretty much summed up the situation we faced at Tan Phu. Our team was glad to discover that not all members of the press who covered the Vietnam War were jerks.

It was also about this time that Sergeant Carey told us one morning at the breakfast table that he wasn't feeling very well. Carey's eyeballs were yellow, and it didn't take a trained medic to figure out that he'd contracted hepatitis, a common illness on American A-detachments. Carey got on a chopper the next day and was evac'd to the hospital in Nha Trang. The primary treatment for hepatitis was simple bed rest and a controlled diet, and we were told he'd probably be back in a few weeks.

Hell! We were now understrength by a third man. We began to run into ourselves coming and going on the nightly guard duties. The B-team said they would send us another medic to replace Dan, but we were told not to expect a replacement for the XO or for Carey.

I found myself spending more and more of my time

helping Martin with the supply duties. There were parachute drops coming in almost every other day as we attempted to replace all the weapons, ammo, and equipment lost on the Le Coeur disaster. With Carey in the hospital, Martin was swamped.

There was also a bubonic plague epidemic in the area around Tan Phu, and every available man on the team was spending part of his time on medical patrols with VandeBerg, pumping antibiotics into the terrified local farmers. One afternoon I gave so many injections that my thumbs gave out, and I had to start pushing home the hypodermic plungers with the palm of my hand.

Occasionally some kind soul back at the B-team would think to throw a few newsmagazines in with our mail from the States. By the time the magazines got to us, they were several weeks old, but we still appreciated finding out about what was going on back in the U.S. There was very little about the war that, from our perspective, was raging in Vietnam. Most of the news was about the civil rights movement and Kennedy's Camelot.

Because we were so shorthanded on the team, we began to send only one man at a time into Saigon for commissary/R&R runs. It was my turn to go in again, but I hadn't had the time to give it much thought. One day Martin and I were out on the DZ, supervising a supply drop, when I happened to see an almost young, Vietnamese peasant woman wander past. She was dressed in the usual ragged, black work clothes, had mud up to her knees, and spit a stream of betel nut juice from her stained mouth as I watched.

"Bill, look at that little cutie," I said, nudging him.

Martin glanced over at her, then looked back at me. "Leigh," he said, "you need a trip to town!"

Chapter 21

The next day, I jumped on the helicopter that dropped in to deliver our mail, and several hours later I was once again in Saigon. I didn't realize how tired I was until I got there. It was late afternoon when I walked into my room at the Annex, locked the door to keep out the curious neighbor girls, tossed my carbine and handbag into the corner, and lay down with my dirty jungle fatigues and muddy boots still on to take a short nap. I didn't wake up until 0600 the next morning.

I felt a lot better when I awoke, and once I'd washed and changed into some civies, I was raring to go. After breakfast on the veranda of the Continental Hotel, I did my PX and commissary chores. By 1100 hours that morning I was done. The bar where Lyn worked was just opening for business, and the bartender told me she wouldn't be in for a while. I left a note asking her to meet me for lunch at a small restaurant we both knew.

As I aimlessly strolled around the tree-lined boulevards, killing time, there was one of those sudden downpours that occur in the tropics. I ducked into the lobby of the Catinat Hotel for a few moments, then the rain stopped all at once and the sun came back out, shining hot from a clear sky. Saigon looked and smelled clean and fresh, all its dirt and sins washed away.

I got to the restaurant right on time, but Lyn wasn't there yet. The place had several empty tables with umbrellas and chairs on the sidewalk out front, and I sat there drinking beer and hoping she would show up. An occasional breeze from the river cooled things a little, and it was very pleasant just to relax and savor still being alive.

When Lyn came walking up, I didn't recognize her at first. I mistook her for a student from the nearby girls' school. Lyn usually wore Western-style clothing, but now she came striding down the sidewalk in a white, Vietnamese *au dai*, complete with a traditional conical straw hat. She had one hand raised gracefully to hold the hat in place. In the other hand, she carried a large bunch of flowers, their stems wrapped in newspaper. She looked simply radiant, and at that instant was the most beautiful woman I'd ever seen.

Tossing the flowers onto the table, Lyn sat down across from me. She was smiling and talking and absolutely bubbling over with good cheer. She was very glad to see me and had been so happy to get the message, she said. Then she started telling me a long rambling story in Vietnamese, English, and French that had to do with how lucky she'd been lately and how good business and life in general was.

The combination of her good mood, the beer, and the weather lifted my spirits almost to giddiness. We ate lunch and talked, laughing often. She wanted to show me her new apartment, but first she wanted to walk a little.

We drifted along the wide, uncrowded sidewalk for a time, then wandered off on smaller streets through a market section. We passed pushcarts full of flowers and small stalls hawking black market items. Lyn bought us snacks to eat from a woman who cooked on a charcoal fire. It was one of those special few hours of life when everything is wonderful and nothing can go wrong.

About four in the afternoon we went to Lyn's new apartment. It was downstairs from her old place, much bigger, and obviously more expensive. While she put her flowers in a vase, I looked around. She had a new TV and a tape player that had both come from the American PX. The furniture looked new, and the paint on the walls was fresh.

"Beaucoup money now," she told me, shaking her head like she couldn't believe her own good fortune. "Beaucoup piasters."

When Lyn went to work at the bar that evening, I waited for her in the apartment. Lyn had an old woman working for her as a maid, and I spent most of my time playing Vietnamese card games with her. She was not only a better player than I, but cheated outrageously, and before Lyn returned at midnight, I'd lost twenty dollars' worth of P's.

The next morning Lyn decided I should go with her to see her family in Cholon. I was surprised at this, but agreed. In those days I was game for about anything.

Her family lived in what you could call a middle-class Cholon neighborhood. Mom and Lyn's younger sisters were lined up by the door to meet us as we went into the ground-floor apartment. Lyn's mother was a little, slightly stooped woman of about fifty. Her hair was pulled back in a bun, and she was wearing the traditional pajama outfit. Her teeth were stained red from betel nut. The two sisters were in their teens and dressed in American-style skirts and blouses. They looked as if they belonged in San Francisco instead of Vietnam.

If any of them were surprised to see me, they didn't let on. Lyn hugged and kissed the three of them while I waited, then she introduced me to them in rapid Vietnamese. We all smiled and bobbed at each other, then went in and sat down.

The sisters were learning English in school and wanted to practice it on me, but Mom, who spoke not a word of English, felt it was her place to be the hostess and entertain me.

As Lyn and her sisters sat across the room catching up on the latest gossip, Mom sat on the couch with me and attempted to communicate. The old woman had spunk, and I could see by the sparkle in her eyes that she saw the humor in this scene. I decided she and I would get along just fine.

Pretty soon Mom told the younger daughter something in Vietnamese and the girl hurried out. She returned in a few minutes with hot tea, and then made several more trips, bringing many odds and ends of food. Mom then went to a cabinet and came back carrying a big family photo album. She took me through it page by page, showing me each photo and narrating in a steady stream of Vietnamese, just as if I were understanding every word.

Lyn had been a cute baby, I noticed. For the first few pages, a man appeared who I thought must be the husband and father. He was missing in later pictures. One page had only a single hand-tinted photo of a young Vietnamese paratrooper. He was wearing the rank of lieutenant.

This was Lyn's brother, I discovered. He was second oldest after Lyn. "Now he stay Hue," Lyn told me. "I no see for almost one year. He too much fight war."

We didn't stay very long, and I kind of hated to leave. Mom was telling me funny stories toward the end, laughing, and reaching over to pat me on the knee. But Lyn, who'd been watching us all night with just the faintest smile, finally came over and pulled me to my feet and out to the waiting taxi. Mom and the two sisters waved to us from the door as we drove off.

"Mama like you," Lyn told me on the way back to her apartment.

In the Saigon bars, I'd noticed there was an entirely different atmosphere since the coup. With the Dragon Lady and her stodgy Victorian morals out of the way, things had loosened up. Occasionally the girls would come out from behind the bar and sit with patrons they liked. Dancing, especially the twist, had been forbidden before, but now all the clubs had small dance areas, and there were couples out on the floor gyrating around everywhere you went. If the coup had confused the peasants around Tan Phu, it didn't seem to have had anything but positive effects in Saigon.

I stayed at Lyn's apartment the entire time I was in Saigon that trip, checking back at the Annex only occasionally to see if my weapon and equipment were still in the corner where I'd dumped them. I had a great time, drank too much, as usual, and wanted to stay longer than my allotted three days. Thanksgiving was quickly approaching, however, and I had most of the supplies we'd need for the large dinner the team planned.

The night before I had to return to camp, Lyn talked more about herself than she usually did, and drank more too. She said she was very proud to be able to send money to her mother and sisters. She was the eldest child and it was her duty. She told me how much she loved her younger brother and said she worried about him all the time and wished there were no war.

I told her that when the war was over, I'd get out of the Army and come back to Vietnam. I was going to get a job with a big American company, make a lot of money, and live in a villa in Saigon. I told Lyn I would help her buy her own bar, and we could take vacations at the beach in Nha Trang or the mountains in Dalat.

We got very excited thinking about this and wove the fantasy on and on into the early-morning hours. We were both dead drunk but happy when we finally went to bed.

I had to get up early the next morning to make it to my 0800 flight back down to Can Tho. I was hungover and grumpy, and so was Lyn.

"Why you make me drink too much!" she snapped as we staggered around her apartment, trying to collect my things. I just grunted for an answer and offered her a couple of Darvon.

Lyn sent the old woman to find a taxi and offered me a cup of the instant coffee I'd bought for her at the PX. I accepted, hoping I could keep it down.

"When you come back Saigon?" Lyn asked, and I gave her the usual answer that I had no idea when or even if I'd ever be back.

"Last night you say you come back Saigon to live in villa and buy me bar," she said, teasing.

"I said I'd do that after we've won the war," I reminded her. "How much longer do you think the war will last?"

She thought about this seriously for a moment. "I think war *fini* in six more month," she told me.

I told her that I would be returning to the U.S. in only a few more months, but that I would try to visit her again before I left. If not then, I said I'd be back when I was a rich civilian. The taxi was out in the street and the driver was impatiently honking the horn. We embraced at her door, and I went back to Tan Phu and the war.

Chapter 22

I got back to camp quicker than anyone expected and was immediately plugged into the guard roster again by a smiling Sergeant Lima. It was business as usual that first night back, with guard shift from 2200 to 2300 hours, a short sleep until 0200, then two hours of the nightly haps. The VC were becoming more and more audacious all the time, and on that night they managed to infiltrate within grenade range of one outpost, killing several strikers and wounding a couple more. Cross was taking care of sending the morning weather report to the B-team, so I got to sleep in until almost 0700.

I woke up groggy and fuzzy-headed, still not recovered from my three days in Saigon, and heard a couple of guys talking next door in the Titis Tavern. "Too bad about old John, I really liked him," I heard someone say.

I immediately thought something had happened to Big John Lowe, our weapons man, and my heart sank. I rolled out of my cot and stumbled into the Tavern to see what was going on. Lowe, Navarro, and a couple of other guys were sitting around the table, listening to our battery-powered civilian radio.

Lowe was obviously not the "John" they were talking

about. "Somebody get hit last night?" I asked, rubbing the sleep out of my eyes.

"Yeah," Navarro said, "the president got greased."

"You mean Diem?" I said, confused.

"No, dumbass, our president—JFK!" someone told me. "He got shot in Dallas."

"No shit," I said, sitting down at the table. "What's for breakfast, Hai?"

I've heard many stories over the years since then from people saying what a traumatic experience it was for them when they found out about the assassination of President Kennedy. For me, in the context of what I'd been through for the last few months, it was no big deal. I mean, hell, people were getting zapped all the time around Tan Phu—people who were friends of mine. Although the Diem murder had impacted us at Tan Phu big-time, I couldn't see how JFK getting bumped off would affect my survival in any way whatsoever.

Hai brought me a bowl of sticky, cold oatmeal with some lukewarm canned milk on it. "You late breakfast," he said, cigarette bobbing in his mouth, ashes flying. "Almost all gone. Too bad, oatmeal now number ten."

"So who killed the pres," I asked, staring down at the disgusting mess Hai had given me, "his wife?"

"Wade, you're an insensitive bastard," Navarro said with a grin.

"Hey, Bill," I said to Martin, "that means we got us a president from your home state, Texas. Why don't you write him and ask him to make sure we get those fucking claymore mines we've had on requisition for four months!"

We started preparing for Thanksgiving. All the A-teams down in IV Corps had been supplied with frozen turkeys, compliments of God-knows-who, and ours was already in our kerosene refrigerator, quickly warming up and approaching the stage of decomposition. Lima and a couple of other guys knew how to make an earth oven that we could fire with charcoal, and they set about constructing it in front of the Titis Tavern.

The day before Thanksgiving a chopper flew in with the mail, and we got the news that our sister team, A-21 at Camp Hiep Hoa, had been overrun the night before.

I'd just been talking with one of the A-21 guys a few days before in Saigon, and he'd told me that things at Hiep Hoa were pretty precarious. He'd said that their LLDB team was particularly rotten, and that the morale on the strike force was very low. Like our detachment at Tan Phu, the Hiep Hoa team was under a lot of pressure from higher headquarters to be more aggressive with their combat operations.

"Christ," the A-21 team member told me, "we're just barely making it from one damn day to the next, and they want us to take our worthless bunch of fucked-up strikers out on extended operations! Shit, we know about half of 'em are VC!"

Now we all sat around the table in the Tavern, listening to the chopper pilot tell us what had happened. Most of his information came from the team's XO, Lieutenant Colby, who had survived the attack. The morning before the attack, Colby reported, the A-21 team leader, Captain Horne, led a platoon-size operation out of camp toward the Cambodian border. Besides the thirty-six strikers, the patrol was also accompanied by half the American A-team and three of the LLDB. The patrol was scheduled to last several days and nights.

Colby had been left to command the camp, which now

was manned by four American Special Forces, nine
LLDB, and 206 strikers. Shortly after midnight Colby
awoke to the sounds of mortar, machine-gun, and small-
arms fire. The commo shack was already on fire, and the
north wall had been abandoned.

By this time VC sympathizers in the striker force had
already killed the guards and taken over one of the
camp's machine-gun bunkers. They turned the gun
around and began mowing down the few, still loyal
strikers who ran from their barracks toward their positions. Two A-21 team members managed to recapture the
machine-gun bunker and hold out for a while until they
were eventually wounded and overwhelmed. The VC
attackers climbed the mud walls of the camp and crossed
the barbed-wire entanglements using scaling ladders. As
they attacked, they yelled in Vietnamese for the strikers
not to shoot, that they only wanted the Americans and the
camp's weapons.

The Cong completely overran the camp, but Lieutenant Colby, though wounded, managed to evade the
enemy in a nearby sugarcane field. The other four Americans, all good friends of ours, were MIA and assumed to
be captives of the VC. These men were: Ike Camacho,
Ken Roraback, Claude McClure, and George Smith.

McClure and Smith had both been members of the
"Barracks Rat" fraternity with us back at Bragg. Smith
was the owner and operator of the infamous Big E, in
which we'd had so much fun roaring around the North
Carolina back roads. Roraback was a radio operator and
had been in my class at Training Group.

At Tan Phu, where we were in a very similar situation,
the most disturbing thing about the battle was the wide-
spread treachery. All but thirty members of the Hiep Hoa

strike force had either refused to fight or had actively aided the VC attackers. The local villagers apparently knew all about the impending attack, but none of them gave warning. A local MAAG-advised Civil Guard unit refused to fire their howitzers in support of the camp.

Although it had been the unofficial rule before the Hiep Hoa attack that no more than two or possibly three Americans should be out of camp at any one time on combat operations, it now became a firm directive. I felt sorry for the survivors of Hiep Hoa, thinking about all the stupid questioning and second-guessing they were now being put through by rear-echelon, political desk jockeys who were themselves terrified of somehow being blamed for the disaster.

Even though we had very little to celebrate at Tan Phu, we went ahead with our Thanksgiving dinner. We invited Phong and the LLDB team, and although they obviously didn't understand this rather esoteric American holiday, they came. They were particularly confused that we would decide to have a big party after we'd recently lost several of our teammates, half the strike force had been wiped out, the presidents of both our countries had been murdered, and more of our friends had just been lost at Hiep Hoa.

"Old American custom," we told them as we stuffed ourselves with the feast.

"Think about Ti-uy Rowe, Bac-si Pitzer, and Pee Hole," Major Phong said, a sad note in his voice. "What they eat today?"

"Yeah," I said, helping myself to another huge serving of turkey, "fish heads and rice for Thanksgiving . . . but remember how Lieutenant Rowe was worried about getting too fat?" I added, trying to find a bright side to all of it. "I'll bet he's really skinny now, huh?"

Down the table I heard someone choke. "You think they're still alive, Major Phong?" I asked.

Phong thought for a moment. "I think Americans still alive," he said. "Pee Hole, I think killed." Phong looked around the table at us with a grim smile. "VC know him and his job at Tan Phu."

The way he said that sent a chill down my spine, and I made a rule to myself right then and there that I would never get involved with the torture of prisoners. I wondered what the VC would do to Phong if they caught him.

There was a lot of leftover turkey, and we gave it all to Hai to take home. He had never tasted turkey before, he told us, and was happy to get it.

I don't know if it was mere coincidence or not, but the VC began their attacks immediately after dark that night and kept it up until daybreak. Seemed to me like they were saying, "Happy Thanksgiving, American capitalist swine!" I wondered what they'd do to help us celebrate Christmas and hoped we'd be out of Tan Phu by then.

Chapter 23

Not long after Thanksgiving the VC developed a new way to harass us at Tan Phu. The enemy had gotten wise to our tactic of using the main trails, all of which paralleled canals, to quickly penetrate their safe areas and take them by surprise. To counter this they began building earthen fortifications on these trails. These berms could be defended at night by small elements of Cong, effectively preventing our patrols from using the routes.

These dirt walls were about one and a half meters high and extended across the trails from the canal bank to the undergrowth on the other side. They were built in series of two or three, each fifty to one hundred meters behind the other. To progress down the trail, each of these strongpoints had to be taken one at a time, because the defenders would abandon the first, fall back to the second, and so on, eventually fading into the night after making a token defense at the last one.

About the only way to storm these positions was by frontal assault, because the flank not protected by the canal was saturated with booby traps and *punji* stakes. The Cong were constructing these positions quite close to camp, so by the time each was successfully overrun, all element of surprise was lost, giving the VC plenty of time to run back toward their safe area in the U Minh.

The actual construction of the mounds was done by the local peasants, supposedly under duress. Our response at Tan Phu was to move down the trails during the day and make the local peasants demolish the fortifications. The poor farmers weren't getting much sleep, having to build mounds all night under supervision of the VC and take them down all day for us.

On one occasion, as a patrol of strikers stood around supervising the destruction of a mound, there was an explosion that killed a laborer and wounded several more. We determined that the VC had booby-trapped the dirt piles by hiding live grenades in them.

After that we began placing charges of TNT in the mounds and blowing them apart prior to ordering the farmers to lug away the displaced dirt. This way, any booby-trapped grenades would be neutralized, the work could progress in a much safer manner, and the peasants wouldn't hate us quite as much.

Late one morning, Martin was preparing to go down the canal on one of these mound-demolition projects, and he asked me if I wanted to go along. These little patrols had become routine, and we had only a couple of squads with us for security. The mounds we were going to remove were only about one kilometer from camp and had evidently been built the night before. It was so close to camp that we didn't even take a PRC-10, which were in short supply, but simply relied on the squad's HT-1 radios for communications with camp.

It was a pleasant morning, and I looked forward to the diversion of getting away from the normal routine chores. During daytime, and that close to camp, there was seldom any enemy contact. Martin and I set off through Tan Phu village in an almost festive mood, as if we were going on a picnic. The strikers felt the same way, especially since they knew they weren't going to be doing any of the physical labor required to destroy the obstacles.

Bill had all his combat gear on and was carrying his M-2 carbine with the taped-together, thirty-round "banana" mags. I hadn't bothered to round up my own equipment and was carrying only my Model 97 riot gun and a pistol. I didn't even have a damn canteen, figuring I'd get a drink at one of the villages if I needed it. This sort of stupidity is what gets people killed, of course, but I was young and still had a lot to learn about war.

It was an easy ten-minute walk down the shady, palm-lined trail. This close to camp, the villagers were mostly friendly, and the strikers talked and joked with them as we strolled along. Several children spotted Martin and me and ran up to us begging for candy, but we had none for them.

We came to the first new mound blocking the trail, and I was a little shocked at how close to camp it was. The damned VC were getting more and more aggressive and fearless all the time. Ever since we'd had our asses kicked back in October, and the Saigon government had zapped Diem, the momentum seemed to have swung more and more in favor of the enemy.

We deployed our two squads in a defensive perimeter, warning them to be careful of booby traps. The local farmers usually disarmed all of these in the morning as soon as the VC left the area so they could safely get to and from their fields, but sometimes the farmers missed one or two.

We sent several men to round up a few villagers for the dismantling detail, then, as the laborers went to work digging the bore holes in the base of the mounds for the blocks of TNT, I sat in the shade with my back against a coconut tree, whittling a stick with my trench knife. The work detail seemed nervous as they worked, and I guessed that they knew the VC had planted a grenade or two.

As I whittled, Martin was busy priming the half-pound blocks of TNT and attaching the time fuses. He walked over to the mound, stuck the handle of a hoe in one of the holes to see if it was deep enough, then told the laborers to get out of the way. They gratefully did so and within seconds had disappeared far down the trail, cowering behind cover.

"Stupid, scared farmers," I muttered smugly to myself. I'd been on these mound-blowing details before and knew that the explosions of two buried TNT blocks didn't amount to a whole lot. I was about twenty-five meters from the mound and figured that was plenty of distance.

Martin placed two half-pound blocks under the mound, pushed some dirt in after them for tamping, and pulled the fuse lighters. "Fire in the hole," he yelled, walking casually back to where I now stood behind the coconut tree. Martin stepped behind another tree next to me and checked the second hand on his watch. "Any time now—" he said.

Kawoooooommm! The earth shook, dropping me to my knees, and the blast tore around the protection of the coconut tree, sucking the breath right out of my lungs. I was completely deafened by the noise and absolutely stunned by the enormity of the explosion. I peered around the tree trunk at the huge, still-smoking crater that now took the place of the mound. I was just starting to ask Bill what kind of TNT he was using when all the dirt clods and rocks that had been blown high in the air suddenly began to rain back down around us. Shit! I had no helmet, of course, and I put my arms over my head, trying to keep from getting brained.

"Holy fuck! What did the VC have in that thing?" Bill asked, face white from the shock.

We made a quick check to see if anyone had been killed or wounded by the blast and were relieved to find out that everyone was all right. This was pure good luck, because the strikers liked to stand out in the open when we blew the mounds to show how brave they were.

A squad leader herded the farmers back up to where we stood around looking down at the smoldering hole in the ground, and he began to scream and yell, berating them for not telling us how big a charge the VC had rigged. Of course, all the farmers maintained innocent expressions and claimed they knew nothing about it. I could tell that several of them were barely holding back smiles, however.

Bill and I agreed that the VC must have planted a couple of dud 155 rounds in the berm, or maybe even a 250-pound bomb from an aircraft. Of course, they couldn't have done it without the knowledge and maybe the assistance of the locals, and this worried me. The fact that they were extending their influence so close to camp was a bad sign.

We left a few of the farmers with their shovels to fill the crater and moved fifty meters down the trail to the only other mound. This time, as the farmers started work on the bore holes, I used the excuse of checking on how the troops were deployed to get farther away from the demolition site. Our interpreter and the two squad leaders walked along with me as I looked things over.

The squads were fanned out in a semicircle, the canal and main trail to their backs. The lush, tropical vegetation that grew next to the canal afforded both concealment and shade for them. I felt a little surge of pride at how well they were positioned, remembering how hopelessly inept they had seemed only a few months before.

We had one A-6 Browning machine gun and two BARs. One of the BARs was manned by Crazy, the constantly smiling striker who had survived the recent big battle without a scratch. Both BARs were in positions that afforded good fields of fire.

After a discussion with the squad leaders, however, we decided the MG should be moved to a different location, where it could better cover the most likely avenue of enemy approach. This pissed the MG crew off because the new position wasn't as cool and shady as their first one, but life's a bitch for a machine-gun crew.

We also had a 60mm mortar team. I was a little upset when I noticed that the mortar was fitted with the small base plate that allowed only handheld operation. The larger base plate and bipod made the weapon much more accurate. At the same time, however, I realized that all that stuff was heavy as hell. By not carrying it, the three-man crew could lug more ammo.

I took the interpreter with me and wandered back toward the canal bank where there were several houses. A few women and kids were out performing their daily chores, and I noticed one of our strikers standing in the middle of the trail nonchalantly taking a leak. The women and kids ignored him.

"Why the hell doesn't he at least hide behind a tree or

something?" I asked the interpreter, irritation in my voice.

The interpreter just shrugged. "They no want to see man piss, they no have to watch," he told me. It made so much sense that I couldn't really argue.

The interpreter went back to check with Martin. I found a nice cool place to sit on the northern end of the perimeter and gazed out over the expanse of open rice paddy. About ten meters to my left I could see the top of Crazy's head as he sat behind his BAR. A little less than a hundred meters to my right front, a small stream ran at a diagonal. There were a couple of houses near it, and the vegetation had been thinned out along the stream's banks somewhat, allowing me to watch what was happening there. I was looking in that direction, trying to spot some pretty, girl farmers, when movement caught my eye.

Several figures in black quickly crossed the clearing and squatted down behind the bank of a low dike. There were four of them, they wore tan sun helmets, and they carried weapons. Because of the angle, the rest of our troops couldn't see them, and they obviously hadn't spotted me sitting quietly in the shadows.

Hot dog, what a great setup! Perfect range for a carbine, I thought to myself. I could probably get all four of the bastards before they even figured out where it was coming from! I think I was actually salivating at the thought of this easy kill. I slowly reached down with my right hand to pick up my weapon, and it was only then I remembered what I was armed with. The fucking shotgun!

I could still see the top of Crazy's head. If I could only catch his attention and somehow get him to crawl over to me, bringing his BAR . . .

"Pssst, Crazy, over here!" I whispered, trying to make enough noise for him to hear but not enough to alert the VC. There was no response.

I found a pebble with my left hand and, still keeping my eyes on the unaware VC, flipped it over at the BAR man with my thumb. . . . Nothing. I found another rock and tried again. This time I heard a click as it bounced off the BAR's stock.

Crazy gave a little giggle and tossed a rock back at me. Hell, the fool thought I just wanted to play games.

Automatic-weapons fire suddenly erupted on the other end of the perimeter and a grenade exploded. This was apparently what the four Cong I was observing were waiting for, because they rose and began firing in our direction. Although I'd flopped down on my stomach at the sound of the first rounds, the VC were still unaware of me.

Crazy ripped off a long burst in the general direction of the enemy. "Kill VC, Trung-si," he yelled at me, "kill beaucoup VC!"

"*Lai day*, Crazy. *Rapide!* Get your stupid ass over here!" I yelled at him. With all the noise of the battle, the four VC didn't hear me and they still crouched in clear view.

"I come, Trung-si," he yelled, finally understanding, and he ran over toward me in a crouch, carrying his BAR by the handle.

"Give me that gun," I yelled, reaching up for it.

Slugs suddenly cracked overhead as the four VC spotted the automatic rifleman and opened up. Crazy saw the enemy at the same time.

"VC die!" he screamed in a rage, running up beside me. Still standing fully erect and firing from the hip, he emptied the rest of the BAR's twenty-round magazine in the general direction of the enemy.

Of course he didn't hit a damned thing, but as he flopped on the ground next to me, an idiotic grin on his face, I patted him on the shoulder anyway. "Number-fucking-one, Crazy, number-fucking-*mot*!"

The four VC were no longer in sight by the time I finally managed to get the message across to the striker that I wanted to shoot his weapon. He gladly turned it over, and I squeezed off a few two- and three-round bursts at likely targets. I looked over at Crazy when I was finished to see if he understood what I was trying to demonstrate, but he just didn't get it.

"No, Trung-si," he corrected me, face serious. "Make go *brrrrrrrrrrrrrrrrrrrt!*"

I heard Martin yelling my name, wondering where the hell I was. I left Crazy where he lay, happily wasting the rest of his ammunition, and ran back to the center of the perimeter. Martin, the interpreter, and the squad leaders had established a command group next to where the 60mm mortar crew were starting to lob off a few HE shells. A striker squatted behind a tree attempting to reach camp on one of the HT-1 radios.

I was surprised at the intensity of the attack and at the large number of enemy involved. Occasionally we'd experienced harassing sniper fire during the day this near to camp, but never anything like this.

I wasn't particularly worried at our situation. The nearness of reinforcement and the capability of getting some fire support from the camp 81s gave me a sense of security. The trouble was, the Vietnamese radio operator wasn't having any luck reaching camp on the HT-1.

"*Mot, hai, ba, bon,*" the man jabbered into the little

plastic radio, occasionally whistling into the mouthpiece instead.

"Where's the other radio?" I asked the interpreter.

"Other radio no have battery," the interpreter told me, his voice full of scorn. "Striker sell battery in village." The HT-1 worked on standard D-cell flashlight batteries, and these were a hot-selling item on the black market.

"He probably traded them for pussy!" Martin yelled at me over the noise of our machine gun, which suddenly began blasting away.

The volume of fire increased up at the end of the perimeter I had recently vacated. I could hear Crazy working out with the BAR, accompanied by several carbines, a Thompson, then the distinctive sound of an enemy K-50 SMG.

One of our troops came running back to us from that end and excitedly reported that the enemy had attempted an assault but was beaten back. We'd taken one killed and several wounded.

I knew that the guys back at camp could hear the battle going on and were probably worried because we had no radio contact. The shooting died down to an occasional single shot or two being exchanged, and we decided to break contact and return to Tan Phu.

All during the short march back to camp I had the feeling we were being sent home with our tails between our legs. There was none of the exhilaration I'd always felt before when returning from a successful operation. The troops seemed subdued too, the only one still in a gay mood being good ol' Crazy, who had fired up every round of ammunition he had and was claiming to have killed many VC.

Chapter 24

Three weeks before Christmas, Carey came back from the hospital. He was twenty pounds lighter and still a little weak, but ready to resume his duties. He brought back the supposedly official word that we definitely would be relieved sometime before the holidays. This was exciting news, of course, because it meant we were suddenly short-timers, with only a couple of weeks left on our tour of duty.

I immediately copped a short-timer's attitude. Ever since the after-action investigation following the battle in October, my usual cynicism and sarcasm had gotten even worse. I suppose that if you added this to my new short-timer persona, I seemed a truly obnoxious bastard those last few weeks at Tan Phu.

I don't know if the VC suspected we were soon to be relieved or not, but it appeared to me they were out to get us before we escaped. The nightly attacks were getting fiercer each time. The Cong were shooting at us constantly now, including during the day. As someone on the team remarked, "If you want to find the enemy around Tan Phu, just stand up!"

We put ourselves on fifty percent alert at night, with half our strike force and half our A-team awake and at our positions at all times. I'd given up ever getting any sleep. There were two big bottles of amphetamine tablets on the table in the Titis Tavern, and we helped ourselves to these as needed to stay awake and alert. After a while even the pills didn't seem to do any good, and we were all walking around like zombies.

The B-team sent us a Sp4. medic named Cooper to help VandeBerg. Cooper fit himself right in at Tan Phu, which meant that after about a week he was as dingbat and wacko as the rest of us. The level of pressure was such during those last few weeks that a man either adapted by getting a little crazy or he broke.

One evening as we sat around outside the Titis Tavern waiting for the sun to go down, Harvey came slithering out to join us. The python had an unusually large bulge, which indicated he'd recently found a real feast some-where. "Any of the villagers' babies missing?" I asked.

There weren't any children missing, but what was missing was even worse—especially for Harvey. Major Phong's pet fighting cock, which he kept tethered outside his quarters, had mysteriously disappeared that morning, and it didn't take much of a detective to figure out the responsible party. Phong didn't say anything to us about it, but he knew that all of us on the American team were laughing our asses off.

A day or two later Harvey also disappeared. We searched all over camp, looking in all his favorite hiding places, but couldn't find the seven-foot reptile. The next morning, when Hai came to fix breakfast, he told us he had found our pet over in the village market. Poor Harvey's rat-catching days were over, Hai told us, as the snake had been skinned and filleted, and was on sale for ten piasters a pound.

Intelligence reports were pouring in again now that Phong was back in camp. Some of these were authentic, but many more were obvious fakes being fed us as psychological warfare. We were getting many confusing reports concerning our missing teammates, some detailing how they'd been tortured to death. Other reports said they were both alive but had renounced the rest of us American capitalist pigs and were fighting for the VC. Another version said that, yes, the Americans were captives and were being treated humanely by the benevolent People's Army.

We also were getting reports about enemy troop strength in the area. One obviously false story that Phong brought over told of how the VC had somehow managed to dig elaborate bunkers, deep in the ground and camouflaged so cleverly that they were almost impossible to find even if you knew where they were. These bunkers were supposedly very near our camp, and although they were within range of the 155s at district, the positions had so much overhead cover that the artillery wouldn't dent them.

"VC in bunkers laugh at 155s," the intelligence report said.

We knew this story was bullshit for a number of reasons. It was obvious that if we couldn't dig deeper than a few feet without hitting water, neither could the enemy. Someone on the team remarked that they'd need an awful big pump to stay dry.

Sergeant Lima, who had been on the receiving end of Red Chinese heavy artillery during the Korean War, was especially amused at the part of the story claiming that "they laugh at 155s."

"Laugh at 155s?" he asked, smiling. "Man, I don't

know *anyone* who laughs at incoming 155s, no matter how deep they're dug in!"

Lima shared something else with us from his past experience, and it didn't do much for team morale. "I wouldn't count too much on this story from HQ that we'll be 'home for Christmas,' " he said. "That's what they were telling us in Korea just before those twenty billion chinks came screaming down on our asses!"

Lima wasn't the only one on the team who cautioned that we shouldn't really count on leaving before Christmas. Adding to the uncertainty of the situation was the fact that we hadn't been given any exact departure date. The vague "before Christmas" could mean anytime from the next day to Christmas Eve. However, the general consensus on the team was that our relief would be there around December 20, and Cross and I drew up a short-timer's calendar reflecting this date, which we kept in the commo bunker.

Time seemed to drag by more and more slowly. We picked up a rumor from the B-team that actually identified the team scheduled to relieve us. "It's supposed to be A-432," our source told us. "Captain DeGracia's the team leader."

The supplies continued to flood in, with several airdrops a week. By this time it had become dangerous even to venture out on the DZ because of the intermittent sniper fire. The planes were taking more and more ground fire too, and it didn't do much for their accuracy with the bundles. One day an entire load of concertina wire went smack into the middle of the main canal. We managed to retrieve some of it, but to recover the rest would have required the aid of Navy divers and a crane. I suspect the wire is still sitting on the canal bottom.

"A-432 is in-country and at Nha Trang right now, being briefed," the intelligence sergeant from the B-team told us one day as he made his rounds of the A-teams on the mail chopper. "They should be here by December eighteen."

"Yeah, if they don't all get killed while they're still at the Alamo with you guys," I said, remembering our own experience there.

When the chopper left and we were alone again, the A-23 team members sat around in the Titis Tavern talking about it. "Figure they get here on December eighteenth like they're supposed to," Lima said, studying the calendar on the wall. "It will take at least two days to brief them and show 'em around. Then figure a couple of days for outprocessing at Can Tho, and another day or two at Nha Trang. . . . Hell, maybe we really will make it home by Christmas."

"Unless the North Vietnamese decide to invade just like the Red Chinese did," said Martin, whose attitude was becoming as pessimistic and sarcastic as mine.

"That means we'll actually be out of this fucked-up place in seven days," someone said, ignoring Martin's remark. We looked around at each other in wonderment. It just didn't seem real.

"We'll need to break out those extra cots for the new guys to sleep on the two days when both teams are here," Lima said. "Tell Hai to buy some extra chow at the market and—" Firing broke out across the canal at the western outpost line. Several stray slugs cracked overhead, and we all instinctively ducked. It was 1300 hours, early in the afternoon.

Needing no orders, we broke up the meeting and rushed to our positions. "Only seven more fucking days,"

I yelled encouragingly to Cross as he ducked in the door of the commo bunker.

Cross and I adjusted our short-timer's calendar to reflect the new departure date and took turns marking off the days. Cross had asked one of the radio operators at the B-team to pass the word to us as soon as A-432 got to their location, and on December 16 this message was tacked on to the end of the daily traffic from HQs:

XXX DETACHMENT A-432 AT THIS LOCATION XXX ETA YOUR LOC 18 DEC XXX MERRY CHRISTMAS XXX

There had been a day or two of relative quiet around Tan Phu, and on the evening before our relief team was to arrive we sat around waiting for dark and hoping it stayed peaceful.

"Maybe we'll just slide right on out of here without ever hearing another shot fired," I ventured.

"What will probably happen is that as soon as we leave, the VC will pull back to the U Minh, there won't *ever* be another shot fired around here, and no one will ever believe us when we tell them how bad it was," Martin said.

"That would be fine with me if they'd just let us alone for the next couple of days," Cross said, voicing what we all felt.

"Wade," Captain Arsenault said later that evening, "I know you won't like to hear this, but you and Navarro will have to go back to Saigon one more time before we leave the country."

"Yessir, can-do, airborne-all-the-way!" I told him, grinning as I snapped to attention and saluted. I bowed, too, just to make sure I'd covered all the bases. "When do we leave, and why?"

"Ponce and Lieutenant Rowe established the commissary and PX accounts in Saigon when you guys got here," the captain said. "So Navarro will have to personally close them out. Our lease is up at the room in the Annex too, and we want to make sure that bill is paid. You're signed for five crypto one-time pads that Nha Trang wants to transfer to a unit in Saigon."

He paused for a moment to build the suspense, then got on with the best part. "Tomorrow, you two jump on one of the choppers that bring in the new team and go take care of it. The rest of us will leave in two days, and we'll meet you up at Nha Trang on December twenty-first."

I had the second shift of stand-to that night from 0200 hours until dawn, and as I looked around the quiet camp, I could hardly believe this was to be my last night there. It appeared that Ponce and I, who were the only two original team members still at Tan Phu who hadn't been wounded, were going to get out of there in one piece after all.

I stepped outside my bunker and stood in the pitch-black night smoking a cigarette. I glanced at my watch and saw that it would be getting light soon. Hai would be starting breakfast in an hour or so, and then—

Thunk-thunk-thunk. I recognized the unmistakable sound of enemy mortar rounds leaving the tube.

"Incoming!" I yelled, alerting the rest of the men, and I jumped back inside the bunker.

The first few enemy rounds landed at the outpost line and in the village. I secretly hoped one of them hit the meat merchant who was selling Harvey. A round burst in the wire and set off a couple of our trip flares, and this started the jittery troops on the wall firing.

As attacks at Tan Phu went, this wasn't much worse than normal. But because I was due to leave the very next day, it seemed worse than it really was. I nervously checked over the BAR and my ammo supply, and checked to make sure the PRC-10 was turned on.

The LLDB were lighting up the sky over the outpost line with illumination from their 81 mortar, and I soon heard Lowe and Navarro's mortar spit out a couple of rounds. The satisfying blast from the HE round's impact soon followed. From the talk I overheard on the radio, the rounds had been very near the target. Lowe adjusted and quickly fired three more times.

Cross notified us that he'd alerted the B-team we were under attack again and that he had them standing by. Arsenault told VandeBerg and Cooper that we'd taken some casualties at Outpost Two up on the north end, and that they were being brought into camp for treatment. A couple of villagers had also been wounded. He told me to be careful not to shoot them if they decided to come across the bridge before daylight.

There was a short lull in the fighting, and I thought it might be all over. Suddenly another trip flare went off in the grove of trees near the front gate. We had two machine guns covering that area and they immediately came roaring to life. There were several explosions that sounded like grenades, but I couldn't tell if our side had thrown them or if they were from the bad guys.

I saw Lima running over in that direction and heard Captain Arsenault, who was up in the watchtower, yelling something down to him. One of our homemade "super claymores" went off with a loud *crack* and bright flash.

"Over to your right, get the bastards!" someone yelled in English, and there was another burst of fire. A round of illumination from one of the 60mm mortars popped over the trees, causing eerie shadows.

The shooting suddenly stopped again, and one by one the positions began calling in their status reports. We had a few more wounded strikers, but no Americans had been hit. Several positions needed more ammo. I reported that there had been no enemy contact at my position and noticed for the first time that the sky had turned pearl-gray and it was almost dawn.

A litter party was coming across the bridge from the village with several wounded, and Hai followed along behind, his usual smile in place and a cigarette dangling from his lips.

"Good morning, Hai!" I yelled at him as he came through the gate. "What's for breakfast?"

"Good morning, Trung-si," Hai answered. "Have number-one oatmeal."

Chapter 25

The distinctive *wop-wop* sound of rotors announced the arrival of incoming choppers, and I'd never heard a sweeter noise. The twelve men of detachment A-432 were only minutes out and were actually an hour earlier than we'd been told to expect them.

There were several HU-1Bs in the flight, and Captain Arsenault was at the LZ to meet them when they landed. I was hurriedly trying to take care of some last-minute commo paperwork with Cross. Navarro stuck his head in the Titis Tavern and asked me if I was ready to go. "Hey, Wade, let's not miss our damned ride! The choppers don't want to shut down their engines."

I barely had time to greet the members of the new team, then was yelling my good-byes to everyone as Ponce and I ran toward the waiting Hueys.

"See you suckers in a day or two," I yelled above the noise of the rotors.

"Hope you catch the clap, you asshole," Martin yelled back.

We circled the camp one time as we climbed up to altitude. Tan Phu looked very peaceful, almost scenic, in the bright morning sunshine. I solemnly gave it my middle finger and settled back for the flight to civilization.

• • •

Since we didn't have our room at the Annex anymore, Navarro suggested we spend our last couple of days in Saigon at the Catinat Hotel right there on Tu Do Street. As usual, we took a cab straight from the airfield. The lobby was crowded with foreign tourists that afternoon, and several of them muttered under their breath in French as Navarro and I walked past them toward the elevator.

I figured that our ragged jungle fatigues, web gear with full combat load, and M-2 carbines just added a little local color. This was, after all, Vietnam.

It was too late in the day to take care of any business, so we decided to clean up and immediately get down to some serious partying. We secured the weapons and crypto pads by sticking them under the mattresses. Twenty minutes later we were on the street. Navarro headed for the Sporting, and I told him I'd be there in a while. I wanted to stop in first and tell Lyn I was in town.

Lyn spotted me as soon as I sat at the bar and she quickly moved down to wait on me. "You say you no come back long time," she said.

"I lucked out," I told her. "I've only got a couple of days. You got anyone staying with you tonight?"

"You know Lyn too ugly, men no like me," she said, straight-faced. "I told you before, you my number-one boyfriend."

"Yeah," I said, smiling. "That's good to hear, because I'm out of money."

"Maybe you only number-eight boyfriend," Lyn replied after short consideration.

We talked for a while, and I bought her a few Saigon teas to keep the bar *mama-san* happy. Business on Tu Do was getting better all the time, Lyn told me. Things were a lot more relaxed since the coup. She said that because it was the start of the long holiday season, which in Saigon began before Christmas and ran through Tet, the town was in an especially festive mood. I gave Lyn a big wad of American money and asked her if she would change it to piasters for me.

Lyn took the money and disappeared into a back room with the *mama-san*. While they were gone I sat gazing out the window. The sun had set and the lights were coming on. Tu Do was filled with Renault taxis, motor scooters, pedicabs, and bicycles. Throngs of people moved along the sidewalks, and there seemed to be many more GIs among them than there had been only a few months before.

Lyn came back and pushed a thick stack of P's across the bar to me. "Mama give you good rate," she told me, "much more than government give." She told me how much was in the pile, and I stuck the money in my pocket without bothering to count it.

I told Lyn I was going to go look around a little, but that I'd be back before closing to take her home. I paid the bar bill, leaving an excessive tip, and wandered out to the street.

Down at the Sporting Bar, I discovered that Navarro had already left, but there were many other guys there whom I knew. I sat with a bunch of rowdies from the 1st Group at one of the little tables that lined the back wall. We swapped war stories and filled each other in on the latest casualties. They'd all heard about Rowe and Pitzer getting captured and wanted to know more about that, and I picked up more details about the battle at Hiep Hoa.

One of the guys suggested we go up the street to a

ritzy nightclub near the Caravelle Hotel. There was a female Vietnamese singer performing there by the name of Bac Yen who was all the rage just then. Three or four of us left and strolled to the club through the warm tropical evening.

The girl had a nice voice, and she alternated singing in Vietnamese, English, and French. The song, "Where Have All the Flowers Gone?" was a popular tune in '63, and Bac Yen sang it half in English and half in French. Considering the time, place, and the performer, the lyrics had special meaning. Half the audience was in tears by the time she got done.

I was throwing my money away as fast as I could and knocking down the drinks as quickly as they arrived. I fell madly in love with the waitress who was bringing them and gave her huge tips for each trip.

It was simply a great night. I was still alive, healthy, and in one piece, and in a few days I'd be out of danger for the first time in six months. Things were getting a little fuzzy by the time the lights in the club were turned up and "last call" was announced. I'd been trying all evening to put the make on the waitress and had forgotten all about Lyn.

I hung around the club pestering the little girl until she finally whispered that she'd meet me out front. The management of the joint frantically herded all of us remaining, hardcore patrons out on the sidewalk, where I waited and waited for the girl. Of course, she never showed up.

The streets were nearly deserted and curfew was only minutes away when I hurried down the street to Lyn's bar. It was closed and Lyn was already gone. Mumbling drunkenly to myself, I staggered as quickly as I could over to her apartment. I knew she'd be mad at me because I'd stood her up, and there was always the chance that she'd decided to take another guy home instead. I said a little prayer as I knocked on her door.

She answered my timid knock almost at once. "Where you go?" she asked me. "I wait and wait. I worry." She had a very stern look on her face, but she let me in.

I drunkenly lied about where I'd been, and she mothered me, helping me get undressed, bathed, and into bed. I asked her for a beer, she told me I'd had enough, and with that I passed out.

"You too sick? Good. Maybe die," Lyn said the next morning as I stumbled out of the bathroom where I'd been suffering a bout of dry heaves.

"Ohhhhh, my head!" I moaned. "Why does everyone hate me?"

"Everyone no hate you. Just Lyn hate," she corrected me. But she brought me some coffee anyway.

By the time I left a few hours later to go find Navarro, I'd groveled my way back into her good graces. When I'd told her I would be making one last trip to the PX that morning, she handed me a long shopping list and made me promise to come straight to her bar as soon as I'd dropped the stuff off in her apartment.

Ponce was back at the Catinat and was brushing his teeth when I knocked on the door. He said he'd had a hell of a night, but appeared to be in a lot better shape than I was. We ate breakfast at the Continental, then took care of closing out our commissary account. A guy in civilian clothes asked me why, if we were leaving the country in a few days, I needed to buy so many cartons of cigarettes and bottles of whiskey. I came up with some lame excuse, and he let me go ahead.

I took a taxi to the villa over on Tran Hung Dao Street where I'd been instructed to turn in the crypto pads and was ushered to the communications center as soon as I got there. The crypto officer had the transfer paperwork already made out, and in a short time the transaction was complete and I was in a cab heading back toward Tu Do.

Lyn took the night off, and we spent a quiet evening at her apartment. Her old servant cooked us a dinner of steak and fried potatoes, and I managed to stay practically sober. Lyn told me she'd been offered a job as manager of another bar just off Tu Do and planned to take it. She said when I came back to Vietnam the next time, I should look for her there.

I promised her I would, although deep down I now had doubts I'd ever return. From the way things had been going at Tan Phu, it looked like the South was losing the war. Although I hoped otherwise, I figured the U.S. would pull out within the year and the communists would take over. This, then, would be my last night in Saigon. I looked around, trying to soak up the exotic Asian atmosphere. It was winter back in the States, and in a few days I'd be there again, living the austere life of a barracks rat.

It was with a good deal of sadness and regret that I kissed Lyn good-bye at her apartment door the next morning and walked through the quiet morning streets back to the Catinat.

Navarro and I flew up to Nha Trang later that day. The other members of A-23 had arrived already, and we found them at the C-team club.

"Oh, look who finally got here," VandeBerg yelled when we walked in. "Hope you had a nice vacation in

Saigon while we were all loading and unloading your damn luggage."

I did feel a little guilty, because Navarro and I had left camp with only small handbags, leaving it to our buddies to make sure the rest of our equipment was taken care of. This had involved loading it on choppers at Tan Phu, unloading it all at Can Tho, then reloading it on a C-123 for the flight to Nha Trang, where, of course, it again had to be unloaded. Since we still had to fly back to Tan Son Nhut to board the homeward-bound KC-135, the process would repeat itself two more times.

The team had completed all the required outprocessing at the C-team by the time Navarro and I got there, so all that remained was for us to turn in the M-2 carbines we'd signed for on our arrival. Nha Trang wasn't really safe in those days, and it felt strange to be walking around with no weapon of any kind. I was glad to hear we'd be leaving the next morning.

The going-home party we threw for ourselves continued all that afternoon. Eventually we moved from the C-team club to downtown Nha Trang and a restaurant/bar on the beach called the Nautique. There, we ran into the survivors of Hiep Hoa, who were flying back on the same aircraft with us, and the party got even wilder.

The Nautique was right on the beautiful beach, and soon we all drifted out to sprawl on the white sand under swaying palm trees. The sun was setting behind us, breakers were rolling in, and as far as I was concerned, life couldn't get much better. Navarro had written a song for the occasion of our leaving, and we sang it together with wild, drunken abandon. It was to the tune of "Give My Regards to Broadway." It went like this:

Give my regards to Saigon, remember me to old
   Tan Phu.
Tell all the boys above the 17th, my tour here will
   soon be through.
Tell 'em of how I'm yearnin' to mingle in the old
   ZI.
Give my regards to Ho Chi Minh, and tell him kiss
   my ass good-bye!

Epilogue

Ship me somewhere east of Suez, where the best is
   like the worst,
Where there aren't no Ten Commandments an' a
   man can raise a thirst. . . .
       —KIPLING

All the survivors of A-23 got back to Fort Bragg without further incident. When the KC-135 landed at Pope, it was late at night, but 5th Group had arranged a little welcome-home for us in one of the old mess halls. The wives and kids of the married guys were there, and it was nice for them.

For us barracks rats, it was about like I'd figured. Fort Bragg seemed especially cold, gray, and desolate after being in the lush tropics. Because it was just before Christmas, practically everyone had already gone on furlough, and this added to the dreariness. I hung around the post until after Christmas Day, then went on furlough myself and traveled back to Tucson to visit my mother and father.

It was good to see them and the few old friends I still had in the area, but all the time I was trying to have fun, I couldn't get Vietnam out of my mind. I found myself wondering what was going on at Tan Phu. How was Crazy, and Phong, and all the troops? And what about Pitzer and Rowe? Somehow I felt like a quitter for coming back home to the good life while there was still a fight going on over there.

After our return, A-23 stayed together as a team. A new medic named Shipley was assigned, who took the place of Pitzer, but we got no new XO. While we'd been at Tan Phu, Special Forces back at Bragg had been busy building a huge demonstration area that was used to show off unconventional-warfare capabilities to various dignitaries. The 7th Group and 5th Group spent all their time either picking up trash on Smoke Bomb Hill or doing construction work on the demonstration area.

Early that spring, A-23 was picked to star in a TV documentary about Special Forces, and we spent about a month on that project. It was actually sort of fun, and at least it got us away from the normal duty rosters and endless shit details.

Bill Martin and I both took the money we'd saved during our six months TDY and bought cars. I purchased a used Austin Healey 3000 roadster, and Bill bought a new Ford sedan. The Healey was the first car I'd ever owned.

Both of our enlistments were about to end, and Bill had already decided to make a career out of the Army. I was undecided and thinking about getting out and going to college, but Martin talked me into re-upping too. For my reenlistment bonus I got $400 in cash and the pick of any place I wanted to go. I asked for reassignment to the 1st SF Group on Okinawa, because I knew that the 1st Group still had primary responsibility for Vietnam.

Bill and I took thirty-day reenlistment furloughs together, driving in our new cars down through Bill's home in San Antonio and then on to Tucson. It was the second time I'd seen my folks in less than four months, and I told them I'd signed on for another enlistment. I think they were actually a little relieved to hear this.

When I got back to Fort Bragg, it was almost summer, and my transfer orders were waiting for me. Before going to Okinawa I was to first attend Thai language school at Monterey, California. I was very pleased to finally be going to the 1st Group, and hoped I'd get at least one last shot at Vietnam before the war was all over.

What Happened to . . . ?

CAPTAIN LEITES. As he'd been promised, getting relieved of his command at Tan Phu had no detrimental effects on Leites's Army career. During the course of the Vietnam War, he returned several more times, served with distinction, and eventually retired as a lieutenant colonel.

LIEUTENANT ROWE. James Rowe was held captive by the Viet Cong for five long years and eventually escaped. After his release, Rowe (then a major) wrote the very popular book *Five Years to Freedom*, about his experiences as a POW. Rowe got out of the Army for a few years during the seventies, then returned in the early eighties, as a lieutenant colonel, to head up the new Army Survival, Evasion, Escape, and Resistance course at Fort Bragg. Rowe later was commander of Training Group, and in the late eighties he was reassigned to the

Philippines, where he was assassinated by communist terrorists.

M.SGT. KEMMER. Kemmer's wrist healed from the wound he received during the mortar attack on the B-team at Can Tho. He served with distinction several more times in Vietnam and was a member of the Son Tay raiding party in North Vietnam.

SFC HARDY. Norm also recovered from his wounds and completed his career in the Army, retiring as a sergeant major.

SFC BROWNING. Browning's prediction of getting his commission reinstated turned out to be correct. The last time I saw Jim was in Vietnam in the mid-sixties, and he was once again a major.

SFC PITZER. Pitzer was held captive with Rowe until 1967, when he was released. Dan worked with Rowe in developing the SEER program and retired as a sergeant major. He died in 1995 after a long illness.

S.SGT. NAVARRO. Navarro went to helicopter flight school not long after we returned to the U.S. from Tan Phu. Navarro finished out his Army career as a chopper pilot, and I recently heard that he was flying a charter service between the islands of Hawaii.

"BIG JOHN" LOWE. John's wounds also successfully healed, and he retired as a sergeant major.

SGT. VANDEBERG. Roger, the ex-Marine, fooled everyone by falling in love, getting married, and getting out of the Army not long after we returned. He attended college, became a history teacher, and taught high school for many years in North Carolina. He also continued his military career as a member of a Special Forces Reserve unit.

S.SGT. CAREY. Ken attended OCS after we got back

and served several more years as a commissioned officer. The last I heard, he'd gotten out of the service and was living in Florida.

SGT. CROSS. Sidney and I remained friends until I transferred to Okinawa. I ran into him again one day in Qui Nhon, Vietnam, in 1965. He told me he was no longer in Special Forces, and I believe he said he was then with the 101st Airborne. We had a good time talking about the "bad old days" at Tan Phu.

PFC/SP4. MARTIN. Bill and I have kept track of each other ever since our days on A-23. Bill served several more tours in Vietnam and was quickly promoted back up through the ranks to First Sergeant. I think it's poetic justice that Bill spent his last couple of years as a "First Shirt" trying to convince young, wild troops that it doesn't pay to do all those very things that he and I liked to do so much. Bill furnished many of the photos for this book and helped jog my memory of those days, now more than thirty years in the past.

CAPT. VERSACE. "Rocky" Versace was held captive for several years with Rowe and Pitzer. He was eventually executed by the VC.

REPORTERS KARALES AND CASTAN. I ran across both these men's bylines many times during the Vietnam War. I'm sorry to say that Castan didn't survive it. From what I understand, Castan was with a unit of the 1st Cavalry in the mid-sixties when they were all overrun and killed.

MAJ. PHONG. After we left him at Tan Phu, Phong continued to advance in his career. I next came across him in 1965 when I was stationed in II Corps at a camp named Vinh Thanh. At that time, Phong had been promoted to Colonel and was the Vietnamese Special Forces

II Corps commander. He came out to visit our camp one day, and we talked about Tan Phu. I asked him about his family, and he said his daughters were going to school in France. Phong had been promoted again the last time I heard of him, in 1970. I don't know if he got out of Vietnam after it fell to the communists.

LYN. I visited Lyn off and on until I left Vietnam for the last time in 1971. She did become manager of her own bar and made a lot of money during the boom years. The last time I saw her, in '71, she told me that business was dropping off considerably as the American troops pulled out. I've always wondered if she made it to the U.S.

CAMP TAN PHU. The Viet Cong continued to put pressure on the camp after we left. From what I've gathered, Special Forces were pulled out of Tan Phu in late '64. The strike force was turned over to district and became an RF/PF unit. Rowe mentions in his book that his captors later took him through the area where Tan Phu once stood and informed him that the camp had been overrun and destroyed. Oddly enough, by 1970 the IV Corps area in the Delta where we once had so much excitement was totally pacified and the safest area in Vietnam.

THE AUTHOR. After Tan Phu, I served four more tours in Vietnam and several years in Thailand with 46th SF Company. In 1965, I was attached to the 173rd Airborne for a few months and pulled another TDY tour with an Okinawa A-team at Camp Vinh Thanh in II Corps. In 1966–67 I was with SOG units and was a cadre at the MACV Recondo School. While with 46th Company in Thailand, 1967–70, I worked with the Thai

Border Police at Hua Hin. In early 1970, I went back to Vietnam and arrived at Camp Dak Pek just in time to be overrun. I spent the rest of that year-long tour helping rebuild the partially destroyed camp and preparing the Yards for the "Vietnamization Program."

During what must have been a fit of temporary insanity, I got out of the Army in 1971, throwing away ten years of active duty and a year and a half of time in grade as a sergeant first class. After ten years of hell trying to be a civilian, I returned to the Army as a member of the AGR program in 1982. I was allowed to retain my old rank of SFC.

Although I went back to a Special Forces unit and returned to jump status, my karma had evidently caught up with me, because I spent the remaining eleven years of my Army career pushing paper and trying to stay out of Army politics. I was not nearly as successful at riding a desk as I'd been at killing commies and was never promoted again. I retired in 1992 at the rank of SFC—with twelve years in grade.

CHAOS, HORROR, AND HEROISM

SPECIAL MEN
A LRP'S RECOLLECTIONS
by Dennis Foley
Author of *Long Range Patrol*

In five years, he went from private to captain,
from New Jersey to Vietnam.
But he always served with the best
the U.S. Army had to offer.

SPECIAL MEN
A LRP'S RECOLLECTIONS
by Dennis Foley

Published by Ivy Books.
Available in your local bookstore.

It began as a war to win—
and ended as a battle to survive.

VIETNAM, 1969–1970
A Company Commander's Journal

by Michael Lee Lanning

At twenty-three, Lanning was made company commander in Vietnam. One hundred men counted on him for their survival.

But lying ahead there would be blood, death, exhaustion, and, finally...pride.

VIETNAM, 1969–1970
A Company Commander's Journal
by Michael Lee Lanning

Published by Ivy Books.
Available in your local bookstore.